United States Marine Corps
Command and Staff College
Marine Corps University
2076 South Street
Marine Corps Combat Development Command
Quantico, Virginia 22134-5068

MASTER OF MILITARY STUDIES

TITLE:
The Balance Sheet of the Battle of Crete:
How Allied Indecision, Bureaucracy, and Pretentiousness Lost the Battle

SUBMITTED IN PARTIAL FULFILLMENT OF THE REQUIREMENTS FOR THE DEGREE
OF MASTER OF MILITARY STUDIES

AUTHOR:
Major Kelsey A. Smith, USA

AY 07-08

Mentor and Oral Defense Committee: Charles D. McKenna, PH.D. Dean of Academics
Approved: _____
Date: 18 APRIL 2008

Oral Defense Committee Member: Craig A. Swanson PhD
Approved: _____
Date: 18 April 2008

Report Documentation Page				Form Approved OMB No. 0704-0188

Public reporting burden for the collection of information is estimated to average 1 hour per response, including the time for reviewing instructions, searching existing data sources, gathering and maintaining the data needed, and completing and reviewing the collection of information. Send comments regarding this burden estimate or any other aspect of this collection of information, including suggestions for reducing this burden, to Washington Headquarters Services, Directorate for Information Operations and Reports, 1215 Jefferson Davis Highway, Suite 1204, Arlington VA 22202-4302. Respondents should be aware that notwithstanding any other provision of law, no person shall be subject to a penalty for failing to comply with a collection of information if it does not display a currently valid OMB control number.

1. REPORT DATE **2008**	2. REPORT TYPE	3. DATES COVERED **00-00-2008 to 00-00-2008**
4. TITLE AND SUBTITLE **The Balance Sheet of the Battle of Crete: How Allied Indecision, Bureaucracy, and Pretentiousness Lost the Battle**		5a. CONTRACT NUMBER
		5b. GRANT NUMBER
		5c. PROGRAM ELEMENT NUMBER
6. AUTHOR(S)		5d. PROJECT NUMBER
		5e. TASK NUMBER
		5f. WORK UNIT NUMBER
7. PERFORMING ORGANIZATION NAME(S) AND ADDRESS(ES) **United States Marine Corps, Command and Staff College, Marine Corps University, 2076 South Street, Marine Corps Combat Development Command, Quantico, VA, 22134-5068**		8. PERFORMING ORGANIZATION REPORT NUMBER
9. SPONSORING/MONITORING AGENCY NAME(S) AND ADDRESS(ES)		10. SPONSOR/MONITOR'S ACRONYM(S)
		11. SPONSOR/MONITOR'S REPORT NUMBER(S)
12. DISTRIBUTION/AVAILABILITY STATEMENT **Approved for public release; distribution unlimited**		
13. SUPPLEMENTARY NOTES		
14. ABSTRACT		
15. SUBJECT TERMS		

16. SECURITY CLASSIFICATION OF:			17. LIMITATION OF ABSTRACT	18. NUMBER OF PAGES	19a. NAME OF RESPONSIBLE PERSON
a. REPORT **unclassified**	b. ABSTRACT **unclassified**	c. THIS PAGE **unclassified**	**Same as Report (SAR)**	**70**	

Standard Form 298 (Rev. 8-98)
Prescribed by ANSI Std Z39-18

Executive Summary

Title: The Balance Sheet of the Battle of Crete, How Allied Indecision, Bureaucracy, and Pretentiousness Lost the Battle

Author: Major Kelsey Aaron Smith, USA

Thesis: The Allied strategy for defending Crete was plagued by a series of compromises at the national and theatre level. The disorder caused by the fractured and often changing strategy made it nearly impossible for subordinate commanders to establish priorities of effort and establish a synchronized operational concept. Consequently, the tactical commander, Freyberg was unable to organize, equip and resource his defense properly.

Discussion: Allied strategy was unsuccessful for two reasons. First, the development of Allied strategy resembled that of a pinball game rather than a deliberative, objectives-based process. Rather than forcing the Germans into a predictable move, counter-move contest, the indecisive Allied strategy caused them to out-maneuver themselves resulting in available Allied combat power not unemployed.
Second, an overall lack of unity of command plagued the implementation of strategies. Politicians, the General Staff and subordinate commanders who disagreed with the strategy did their best to derail or not support it. Not only were the Allies strategically out maneuvered due to these factors, but the consequences of these strategic errors were visited on operational and tactical units in dramatic fashion.
The operational commanders tasked to provide forces, equipment, resources and support to the effort considered Greece and eventually Crete economy of force operations and released resources without reducing their own capabilities.

Conclusion: The Allies failed to clearly define, articulate and implement the strategic objectives of their entry into Greece. As a result, subordinate commanders were unable to create operational level unity of command and synchronize their efforts to achieve the Allied objectives. Consequently, CreForce and its commander were unable to obtain, organize and synchronize the elements of combat power necessary to defend Crete and lost the battle.

DISCLAIMER

THE OPINIONS AND CONCLUSIONS EXPRESSED HEREIN ARE THOSE OF THE INDIVIDUAL STUDENT AUTHOR AND DO NOT NECESSARILY REPRESENT THE VIEWS OF EITHER THE MARINE CORPS COMMAND AND STAFF COLLEGE OR ANY OTHER GOVERNMENTAL AGENCY. REFERENCES TO THIS STUDY SHOULD INCLUDE THE FOREGOING STATEMENT.

QUOTATION FROM, ABSTRACTION FROM, OR REPRODUCTION OF ALL OR ANY PART OF THIS DOCUMENT IS PERMITTED PROVIDED PROPER ACKNOWLEDGEMENT IS MADE.

Preface

My first experience with the island of Crete occured late in 2003. I had just returned from Iraq and my family and I took a vacation to the island for a little rest and relaxation. We expected a tropical island paradise, but were rewarded with a clash of civilizations, suicidal drivers (worse than Italy), oppressive heat, and European accommodations at a German resort. Thankfully, we had been living in Europe for the past three years and were not entirely shell-shocked by our initial experience. After overcoming our broken expectations, we ventured out to experience the beautiful beaches, eclectic villages, odorous Europeans, and scenic mountain vistas. What struck me then, while attempting to find interesting places to visit while thumbing through a brochure written in German, was how unprepared for this trip I was. I knew nothing of Crete's history, the culture, let alone what attractions we might want to see. This paper has been opportunity to make up for that ignorance. My only regret is that I am unlikely to repeat my visit. There are just too many other vacation spots more attractive for family vacations. However, I have appreciated the opportunity to broaden my knowledge and give Crete a second chance to make a first impression. Since starting this project I have seen Crete through the eyes of photographers, soldiers, tourists, and ancient and modern authors alike; it has been a rewarding experience. Of course, this paper represents all too many hours of reading and writing that could not have been possible without the patience and encouragement of my wife, Natalie. She has done more than her share of entertaining and distracting our two boys, Kale and Lincoln, who have fortunately become accustomed to daddy's abundance of family time.

Table of Contents

	Pages
EXECUTIVE SUMMARY	ii
DISCLAIMER	iii
PREFACE	iv

INTRODUCTION
- The Struggle for the Mediterranean 1
- Crete by Accident 2

BACKGROUND
- Allied Strategy in the Mediterranean 3
- The Axis Position and Mussolini 4

STRATEGIC CONFUSION
- Defending Greece 7

OPERATIONAL INDECISION 8

PREPARATIONS
- Retreat from Greece 9
- Developing the Defense 10
- Engaging the Population 13

TACTICAL DISPOSITIONS
- Cunningham and the Royal Navy 14
- The Royal Air Force 15
- CreForce Headquarters 16

INTELLIGENCE 17

THE DEFENSE 18

THE RESULTS 20

CONCLUSION 21

APPENDIX A
- Maps of Crete 24

APPENDIX B
- Crete and the Mediterranean 25

Table of Contents

Pages

APPENDIX C
    Reinforcements Intercepted 26

APPENDIX D
    Air Bases in the Easter Mediterranean 27

APPENDIX E
    Aircraft Ranges 28

APPENDIX F
    Allied Chain of Command 29

APPENDIX G
    German Chain of Command and CreForce Commanders 30

APPENDIX H
    Allied Defense Sectors 31

APPENDIX I
    Suda Sector and Fixed Defense 32

APPENDIX J
    Suda and Canea Sectors 33

APPENDIX K
    Canea Sector 34

APPENDIX L
    Maleme Sector 35

APPENDIX M
    Heraklion Sector 37

APPENDIX N
    Retimo 39

APPENDIX O
    CreForce Task Organization 41

APPENDIX P
    Suda Sector Task Organization 42

Table of Contents

Pages

APPENDIX Q
Canea and Maleme Sector Task Organization 43

APPENDIX R
Retimo and Heraklion Sector Task Organization 44

APPENDIX S
Operation Mercury 45

APPENDIX T
Attack Maps 46

APPENDIX U
Royal Navy Defense 48

APPENDIX V
Royal Navy Loses 49

APPENDIX W
German Forced Landings on Maleme 51

APPENDIX X
Cretan Resistance and the SOE 52

APPENDIX Y
A Sketch of Major General Sir Bernard Cyril Freyberg's Leadership 53

NOTES 56

BIBLIOGRAPHY 63

INTRODUCTION

In late 1940 the land battles of World War II accidentally came to the Mediterranean. Nazi Germany had recently prevailed over the Allies and accepted the French surrender, was wrapping up its unsuccessful Battle of Britain and was preparing for Operation Barbarossa, Hitler's attempt to defeat Russia. To that time, Hitler and Germany were prepared to deal diplomatically with the Balkan and eastern Mediterranean states so long as Britain recognized their neutrality.[1] The Allies, namely Britain and the Commonwealth, were satisfied with their position in the Mediterranean but were struggling to rebuild combat power while attempting to solidify control of the Middle East and northern Africa. Neither Germany nor the Allies had designs for the eastern Mediterranean. Enter Benito Mussolini and the "hapless Italian Army."[1] On 28 October 1940, Italy marched into Greece and precipitated what would become the Battle for Crete (APPENDICES A and B).

The Italian failure to conquer Greece and subsequent collapse into Albania brought together the two unwilling belligerents, Germany and the Allies. Germany was forced to delay its attack on Russia in order to solidify its southern flank, and the Allies cobbled together forces to protect their Mediterranean sea lanes. Embroldened by earlier successes and armed with combat power to spare, Germany executed a deliberate bid for the region, and the Island of Crete. "Muddling along in typical fashion,"[2] the Allies squandered time, opportunity and combat power, first in Greece, then on their primary objective Crete.

A cursory study of the Battle of Crete might suggest that the German Army was a better-trained force, that Germany could more quickly generate combat power, and that it could project that combat power more swiftly than its Allied opponents could. However, a more accurate depiction of the result is that the outcome on Crete was more a result of Allied failures than German success.

Allied strategy was unsuccessful for two reasons. First, the development of Allied strategy resembled that of a pinball game rather than a deliberative, objectives-based process. Rather than forcing the Germans into a predictable move, counter-move contest, the indecisive Allied strategy caused them to out-maneuver themselves, resulting in available Allied combat power not being unemployed.

Second, an overall lack of unity of command plagued the implementation of strategies. Politicians, the General Staff and subordinate commanders who disagreed with the strategy did their best to derail or not support it.[3] Not only were the Allies strategically out maneuvered due to these factors, but the consequences of these strategic errors were visited on operational and tactical units in dramatic fashion. Equipment and supplies needed in theatre were scarce, yet were stockpiled at both the strategic and operational level in order to prepare for unplanned contingencies.[4] Services operating in the same theatre were concerned with the achievement of service-oriented objectives rather than cooperating to achieve theatre objectives.[5] Even when reallocation of resources was implicitly directed, commanders did so only if the loss did not threaten operations they deemed more important.[7]

Not withstanding the strategic inconsistencies and the resulting operational and tactical complications, CreForce, the headquarters designation for Allied forces on Crete, did hold significant operational/tactical advantages that should have buoyed their efforts. CreForce had more than six months to prepare their defense,[8] the Royal Navy retained maritime supremacy of the Mediterranean,[9] CreForce outnumbered their attackers,[10] the Cretan population was friendly to the Allies and actively resisted the Axis invasion,[11] the Allies benefited from better logistical arrangements and interior lines of communication, and the Axis was unable to provide adequate reinforcements. At battle's end, Axis casualties were triple the Allies, the *Luftwaffe* had lost 30 percent of the planes involved,[12] the Allied naval blockade was successful,[13] and only one Axis objective – Maleme Airfield - was actually seized, the remainder were occupied during Allied retirements. Yet, ten days after the battle began the Allies retreated from Crete leaving the battered XI *Fliegerkorps* bewildered yet in control of the island.[14]

Rather than assume that the Germans fielded a more formidable fighting force and were more capable of projecting that force, a more careful study will show that CreForce was unable to synchronize the elements of combat power. More significantly, because they failed to take advantage of precious and confirmed intelligence, the Allies miss-identified the objective of the German assault, did not mass forces to deny the German objectives, and fought an economy of force operation rather than a determined defense due to a lack of unity of command.

BACKGROUND

By 22 June 1940 Great Britain and the Commonwealth were the only remaining combatants left to represent the Allies.[15] Unable to gain a foothold in Europe, the Allies concentrated on gaining superiority of the Atlantic Ocean and maintaining superiority of the Mediterranean Sea.

Key to maintaining control of the Mediterranean were the Allied bases at Gibraltar, Alexandria, and the island fortress of Malta.[16] Although strategically placed in the center of the Mediterranean, Crete was not considered significant so long as Greece remained neutral. However, as early as May 1940, First Lord of the Admiralty A.V. Alexander proposed, "seizing the initiative and [occupying] Crete."[17] Alexander's intent was to pressure Mussolini into accepting the British appeal for Italian neutrality. Britain's new Prime Minister, Sir Winston Churchill, denied Alexander's proposal because a British presence on Crete would compromise Greek neutrality.[18] Therefore, Allied occupation of Suda Bay would only occur in the event of an Italian invasion.[19]

Allied ground forces regrouped in Great Britain following the Battle of Britain and successfully denied a German crossing of the English Channel. Other Allied forces consolidated gains in India and Southeast Asia. Remaining Allied operations occurred in North Africa and Egypt where C-in-C Middle East, General Archibald Percival Wavell, battled the Italian Tenth Army to retain control of Alexandria, the Suez Canal, Cairo, and Palestine.[20]

Although Allied Air and Naval Forces denied the Axis channel crossing, Adolph Hitler was confident the British were incapable of regaining a western European foothold. With his rear –western Europe- secure, Hitler continued to set the conditions for Operation Barbarossa. As outlined in his book, *Mein Kampf*, Hitler's Operation Barbarossa would reclaim western Russia from the Soviets. To do so, it was essential that Hitler secure his right flank, southeast Europe.

Hitler wished to protect the Balkans from either political or military involvement in order to reap the best possible economic benefits. He reasoned that use of any military force would provoke meddling from the Allies or cause Soviet intervention – particularly in the Romanian oil fields - and endanger the success of Operation Barbarossa.[21] Hitler thought that if the Balkans remained unmolested until Barbarossa began they would have no viable economic or diplomatic options other than to support the Axis.[22]

Italian Dictator Benito Mussolini viewed the Mediterranean "as his private Italian lake,"[23] an illusion Hitler willingly encouraged because the *Kriegsmarine* had no warships of note in the

Mediterranean.[24] By encouraging Mussolini's escapades in the Mediterranean and supporting Italian expeditions in Africa, Hitler offered the Allies significant distractions. These distractions tied the Allied Middle East forces to the defense of Palestine and Egypt lest they risk losing control of the Suez Canal. Germany was then free to manipulate the Balkans in preparation for Barbarossa without fear of an Allied threat to his flank. Hitler's Italian distraction in Africa completed the *fait accompli* and isolated the Allies outside of mainland Europe.

On 28 October 1940, thwarted by German designs for Yugoslavia and unquenched by his latest acquisition of Albania, *Il Duce* (Mussolini) sent General Metaxas, the Greek Prime Minister, an ultimatum.[25] Rejecting the Italian ultimatum threw Greece into war with Italy. Mussolini's blundering, ill-conceived expectations of a "triumphal march"[26] evaporated. The Greek Army, supported by Greek reservists, men, women and children met the Italian Army in the mountains of northern Greece and stopped the Italians cold. The Allies immediately offered military assistance to combat the Italians. Metaxas, sensing less than an altruistic offer declined large-scale assistance but accepted British Air Force support coupled with meager number of troops.[27] The presence of even the meager British foothold immediately concerned Berlin.[28]

Metaxas also authorized Admiral Andrew B.Cunningham, CinC British Mediterranean Fleet, to occupy Crete. British ships, aircraft, and advanced parties of the Allied Brigade (14th Infantry Brigade) began to arrive in Crete 48 hours later.[29] Metaxas requested that the Allies further garrison Crete in order to allow him to reinforce Greece with his Cretan divisions. These actions set in motion the accident that was to become the Battle of Crete.

By early winter 1940, Greek Forces had pushed the Italians into Albania. Meanwhile, in Africa Wavell's Middle East forces manhandled the numerically superior Italians. Fearing collapse of his southern perimeter and a possible threat to the Romanian oil fields, Hitler issued the Axis orders to invade Yugoslavia and Greece. In concert, he deployed Field Marshal Erwin Rommel and the *Deutsches Afrika Korps* to Africa to aid the bumbling Italians.[30]

STRATEGIC CONFUSION

Ultra[31] alerted the Allies to Hitler's plan to invade Greece. The threat of a German invasion of Greece forced Churchill and the British General Staff to develop a strategy for maintaining their position. The Allies wished to protect Egypt as well as their foothold on the European continent and requested that Metaxas allow them to provide assistance. Metaxas denied the request, judging that the force Wavell offered was a token and would further provoke the Germans.[32] Instead, he requested that the Allies assist him with air and naval support from Crete. The Allies continued to press and on 29 January 1941 the new Greek Prime Minister, Alexander Koryzis, accepted British assistance "in any quantity."[33]

The Allied strategy was very fractured. Churchill believed it necessary to support Greece at the expense of offensive operations in Africa.[34] By defending Greece, the Allies would be able to strike at German holdings in Romania and the Balkans.[35] This demonstration of Allied resolve would likely win Turkish support. Turkish support would strengthen the Allied hold in Palestine, Iraq and Egypt and guarantee security of the Suez.[36]

Sir John Dill, the Chief of the Imperial General Staff, and the other Chiefs of Staff believed the best Allied efforts could be made by consolidating forces in Egypt and concentrating on the development and defense of Crete for Allied purposes – as a Air and Naval Base in the Mediterranean.[37]

It is difficult to discern which option would have better countered the German designs; instead of fully implementing one or the other, the Allies compromised. Churchill dispatched

Wavell to Greece with orders to establish support for mainland Greece and set up Crete's defense. The solution Wavell implemented was not suitable for anything, other than to safeguard his position in Africa.

The two Allied divisions and four air squadrons were not enough to stop the Axis invasion of Greece on 6 April 1941. At the request of the Greek Government, in order to spare the country further devastation, the Allies evacuated Greece beginning 24 April 1941.[38] Thus, Churchill's strategy became untenable.

The Allied Chiefs of Staff failed to provide proper resources to support the Greek defenders and did not enforce their will on their subordinate commander, C-in-C Middle East, General Wavell. Churchill frequently questioned why the effort was not receiving necessary support.[39] On 12 November 1940 the Allies telegraphed Athens that their requests were unsupportable. However, on further inspection, it appears that the British Chiefs of Staffs were only willing to part with 1 percent of the surpluses available. Athens was told that out of the 1,100 anti-tank guns available only eight could be spared, and out of the 700 Bofors anti-aircraft guns on-hand, only twelve could be spared, although 100 were being produced monthly.[40] At Churchill's insistence the Chiefs of Staff reevaluated their allocations and impressed upon Wavell a list of resources he would allocate to Greece.[41]

Wavell disagreed with the Chiefs and Churchill and on many occasions argued "if we allow the Greek and Cretan commitments to grow any further at the expense of Egypt we shall risk our whole position."[42] The Allied strategic concepts laid out by Churchill and Wavell's concern for his own strength in Egypt could not be reconciled.[43] The inability of the Chiefs to arbitrate further complicated future developments. Their 12 November allocation instructions designated that 20 Hurricanes from Malta be relocated to Greece. Wavell answered, "I cannot approve the 20 Hurricanes going to Greece,"[44] instead he transferred them to Egypt buttressing his forces. Of the 300,000 personnel available to Wavell,[45] only two divisions were dispatched to Greece and a Brigade of 2500 men was dispatched to Crete.[46] Of the 1000 aircraft, 1000 pilots and 16,000 air support personnel available in theatre only four aging squadrons assisted Greece.[47] Six total aircraft were to defend Crete, three Glouster Gladiators and three Blenheim Bombers.

At the conclusion of the Battle of Greece, the aforementioned strategic compromises and inadequate apportionment of strategic resources paved the way to Greek capitulation and set the conditions to ensure the Axis and Allied collision at Crete. When agreeing to the retreat from Greece, Churchill impressed upon the Chiefs and Wavell that in order to preserve the holdings in Egypt and Africa, "[Crete] must be stubbornly defended."[48] The defense of Crete would now test the stratagem of Sir John Dill and the Chiefs of Staff.

OPERATIONAL INDECISION

Continued bickering at strategic levels plagued the orderly withdrawal of Allied forces from Greece and complicated any semblance of an efficient transition to the defenses of Crete. Strategic divisions within Churchill's Cabinet, the Chiefs of Staff and the Theatre commander would now directly influence the defense of Crete. Churchill directed that the Allies hold Crete at all costs, the Service Chiefs attempted to strengthen other Mediterranean positions, and Gen Wavell planned to return the troops to Alexandria and Africa. These contradictory approaches understandably created operational friction. Units arriving at ports would believe themselves to be embarking for Alexandria only to find the ships were destined for Crete. Likewise, ships would embark troops for Crete and deliver them to Alexandria. Only Churchill's direct intervention brought focus to the melee. He eventually directed that Crete would be the priority for all units leaving Greece.[49]

PREPARATIONS

Further complicating the withdrawal of forces from Greece was the availability of proper transports. Admiral Cunningham's Royal Navy faced immeasurable difficulties throughout the Mediterranean due to a lack of Allied air cover. The Royal Navy remained unopposed by the Italian Fleet or *Kriegsmarine*. However, the unchallenged *Luftwaffe* made littoral and naval escort operations dangerous.[50]

In response, the Royal Navy evacuated forces using armed combatants and small, fast troopships instead of larger, more vulnerable, troop and merchant ships. The warships were much more capable of defending themselves. However, their holds and decks often could not accommodate the large machinery of war, forcing commanders to either destroy or abandon it. If the heavy equipment did make it to the quays, some overzealous embarkation officers, enforcing the GHQ Middle East order, "arms should not take precedence over men," demanded that troops discard even their rifles.[51] This resulted in units arriving on the quays in Suda Bay minus their special equipment (howitzers, mortars, and trucks) and subsequently being utilized as infantry. From CreForce's perspective, the addition of the combat forces was welcome. However, the missing capabilities would leave holes in the defenses. The reduced capacities of the warships not only required leaving behind equipment but also threatened the integrity of units. Often units, specifically the 2nd New Zealand Division, Lieutenant-General Sir Bernard Cyril Freyberg's Division, embarked on vessels bound for different ports, geographically separating the force. Though not purposeful, these practices reduced moral and combat

combat effectiveness. Compounding this issue were the individual soldiers and small unit leaders who elected to speed their withdrawal and left equipment strewn along the Greek roads. These individuals and units embarked ships, sometimes without individual weapons, leaving irreplaceable equipment left behind.[52]

Units arriving on Crete did not occupy prepared defenses and areas of operation, even though the Allies had occupied Crete six months before.[53] Until Churchill declared that Crete would be defended it seems that the purpose of Allied forces on Crete had been unclear. In addition to London's initial lack of strategic priority towards Crete, Gen Wavell prioritized personnel and resources first to the Middle East Theatre, the Western Desert, and Greece.[54] As Crete was included in his theatre, in November 1940, Gen Wavell deployed the 14 British Brigade to safeguard Crete from Italian forces based on Rhodes.[55]

14 Brigade clearly remained a garrison force that allowed the Greek Government to transfer the Cretan Infantry Division to the Greek mainland but did little to improve the defensibility of the island.[56] Contributing to this failure was the command turnover; in six months from November 1940 to April 1941 there were seven commanders (APPENDIX G) of the Crete garrison. The constant turnover surely hindered long-term preparations, anticipation of contingencies and the continuity of ideas.[57] The lack of vision and drive[58] exhibited by his predecessors and passed down to Gen Freyberg likely did the most to handicap the defense.

Although little was actually accomplished prior to Gen Freyberg (APPENDIX Y) assuming command of CreForce, two important processes had begun; defensive outlines were prepared, and manning requirements were hammered out. The initial garrison commander and commander of 14 Brigade, Brigadier O.H. Tidbury, conducted a thorough evaluation of the island's natural defenses and outlined to Wavell his plan to build Crete into a "second Scapa."[59]

He envisioned German airborne landings at Malame, Retimo and Heraklion airfields but developed his defensive plans around Suda Bay. Wavell, with the desert offensive pending, disagreed with Tidbury's assessment and believed that the island could be defended with a small force.[60] Tidbury's defensive architecture was carried forward until Freyberg arrived, but would be overlooked even though Ultra signals continued to suggest an airborne invasion.[61] Tidbury was replaced in January 1940 and the garrison accomplished little in the intervening months as four subsequent commanders rotated in and out monthly.[62]

The defensive plans for Crete continued to languish until Major-General E.C. Weston prepared to reinforce 14 Brigade with his MNBDO, Mobile Naval Base Defense Organization. Arriving on Crete before the MNBDO, the Royal Marine General assessed that he would require three fresh and fully equipped brigade groups to defend the fleet and air bases, and defend the island against invasion in the event of a German victory in Greece. In addition, Gen Weston petitioned Wavell for additional air defense batteries and increasing the fighter presence on the island to three squadrons. The Middle East Joint Planning Staff agreed with Gen Weston's assessment but needed all available troops to defeat the Axis offensive in the Western Desert and RAF Middle East would not release the aircraft. The planning staff's final solution was to evacuate all troops from Greece to Egypt, replace units in Egypt, and send the fresh units to Crete.[63] Why fresh units were not sent to Crete as others were evacuated from Greece remains unclear. However, the juggling that resulted, as earlier described, did not produce fresh troops on Crete, severed habitual command relationships, and created confusion for army commanders as well as caused the Royal Navy to expand their already Herculean task.

As was the case in the air over Greece and the Mediterranean, the Royal Air Force (RAF) Middle East continued relatively uncommitted outside of Egypt, Iraq and North Africa. In addition to perceived[64] limited resources, providing air support to CreForce was complicated by geographic and infrastructure complexities and hindered by command relationships (APPENDIX F).

The RAF commanded the assets allocated to support CreForce. Likewise, their integration required the approval of RAF Middle East. Because the airfields were central to CreForce's defensive plan this arrangement created operational complications. Recognizing this shortcoming, the RAF sent Group Captain G.R. Beamish to coordinate RAF support to the island. Beamish found the airfields ill sited, under construction and unable to support sufficient aircraft maintenance and support personnel.[65] The fact that the RAF was responsible for the construction of its own airfields and the absence of RAF coordination in the early stages left air assets in an unfavorable disposition.[66]

Both Maleme and Heraklion, the usable aerodromes, sat on the northern coast of Crete. Due to their location, the aircraft on the fields could not benefit from the protection of the southern mountains and would be at the suspected epicenter of the German assault. Additionally, any ground based air defense of the airfields would be located to the south and afford the Germans the opportunity to attack before coming under effective fires. Had the RAF had the time or inclination they ought to have built airstrips on the plateaus of the mountains.[67] The relative security of the mountains would have allowed the RAF to deploy a greater number of aircraft in support of the Cretan defense, design an overlapping defensive umbrella and provide adequate facilities for maintenance and support personnel.

Rather than take on the task of expanding and improving the supporting infrastructure, and deploying extensive maintenance and support personnel to Crete, RAF Middle East elected to use the exposed airfields and rotate aircraft to and from Alexandria. Once the Germans began early probing attacks it became obvious that the RAF position was untenable. Aircraft were destroyed before they could be launched and those that managed to get airborne could not land during the attacks. Thus, the presence on Crete was not capable of fending off the determined attacks against the airfields and the RAF withdrew all aircraft from Crete even before the German invasion (Operation Mercury, APPENDIX S) began. Likewise, the *Luftwaffe* remained unchallenged over Crete (APPENDIX E) and was successful in confining the Royal Navy to waters south of Crete and providing constant close air support to the *Fallschirmjäger* of the XI *Fliegerkorps*.[68]

Early preparations of the Cretan defenses were successful in one area. Unfortunately, its capabilities seem to have been largely unexploited and therefore unmeasured. As early as October 1940, the British SOE, Special Operations Executive – formerly the MI(R), Military Intelligence (Research) – began operations on the island of Crete. Initially SOE, *Churchill's Secret Army*, conducted reconnaissance and gathered intelligence in case the Allies found it necessary to occupy Crete. Once the Allies were invited, the SOE began to expand their operations considerably. Rather than conducting covert reconnaissance, the SOE engaged the Cretan population. Their purpose was three fold. They were to organize and train the local militias, prepare a resistance network of influential civilians in the case Crete was lost, and prepare an escape plan for the Greek King if his evacuation became necessary.

Once it appeared the German attack could be successful, Freyberg ordered the evacuation of King George of Hellenes to Alexandria. He was successfully ushered through the mountains and network of villages in central and southern Crete to the HMS *Decoy* and *Hero*[69] off the southern coast, by a collection of SOE-trained militia and either a platoon of Royal Marines[70] or a platoon of 18th NZ Battalion Infantry.[71]

The success of the SOE efforts to train the local militias and Cretan civilians is difficult to measure. However, Cretan Reservists, militia, and civilians proved invaluable in the static defenses, and in searching out and destroying isolated *Fallschirmjäger*.[72] Freyberg's only attempt to utilize these indigenous patriots was to break apart their habitual command structure and place them under the command of his regional commanders. The regional commanders reluctantly accepted their charges and often viewed the Cretans as "ill trained, ill equipped rabble."[73] Worse yet, Allied commanders refused to improve the arms of the Cretans with Allied surpluses available.[74]

As hobbled as they were by the Allies, the Cretans proved to be vicious, determined and ingenious. Cretan soldiers and civilians regularly attacked and destroyed German formations with the weapons at hand (rocks, shovels, ancient rifles and sharp instruments) and then put the German weaponry to work against the Germans.[75] Would the defense of Crete have been successful if Freyberg and his pretentious commanders courted the population, and properly armed and integrated the Cretan Reserves? While the answer to that question is impossible to know, the Cretan population violently opposed the German invasion and resulting occupation. (APPENDIX X)

TACTICAL DISPOSITIONS

By 30 April 1941, the day GEN Freyberg assumed command of CreForce, the major operational movements were complete. The Royal Navy had nearly completed the colossal task of transferring troops from Greece to Crete at great expense to men and ships. Though the Navy losses to date were extensive (APPENDIX V), Adm Cunningham and his Royal Navy would buttress the CreForce defense.

Adm. Cunningham's ships continued to provide the defense with supplies and equipment, they continued to screen the island, and conduct limited attacks.[76] The *Luftwaffe* threat degraded the Navy' ability to maintain a screen and required Adm. Cunningham to position his ships to identify and track the German amphibious fleet during the day and then close and destroy it at night. This practice netted three German amphibious reinforcement attempts, destroying 4,000-6,000 reinforcements from the 5th *Gebirgs* Division and caused the Germans to cease amphibious reinforcement attempts.[77]

In an attempt to even the odds and reduce the *Luftwaffe's* air attacks, Cunningham twice bombarded Scarpanto and once the Maleme airfield.[78] These attempts to reduce the dominance of the *Lutfwaffe* had little effect, but did demonstrate to all the resolve and extent to which the Royal Navy was attempting to support the defense (APPENDIX U).

Freyberg would benefit little from what RAF assets he inherited but would soon observe the effects of an unchallenged Luftwaffe. As previously mentioned, the Air Force did little to prepare for or provide for the defense of Crete. They did work to improve the existing airfields on the northern coast, during the initial occupation. After the German "Shock and Awe" campaign began on 14 May 1941, the Air Force lost three of its six aircraft and withdrew the surviving aircraft to Egypt. On 23 May, Air Marshal Arthur Longmore, CinC RAF Middle East, made a final attempt re-establish a presence over Crete. En route, the 12 Hurricanes encountered the Royal Navy and lost two to a fratricide incident illustrating the lack of operational coordination. With the remaining aircraft destroyed over Crete, further attempts were considered foolish and control of the sky was ceded to the *Luftwaffe*.[79]

With the Royal Navy supporting as best it could muster but trapped at sea and the RAF abandoning CreForce to the clutches of the *Luftwaffe*, Gen Freyberg fought the German onslaught with the CreForce he had. To date CreForce numbered approximately 30,000 men composed of 14th Brigade, MNBDO, 2nd New Zealand Division, and 19th Australian Infantry Brigade. In addition to the Allied troops, King George placed all Greek commands under CreForce command increasing Freyberg's available strength by approximately 10,000 and nine Regiments (APPENDIX O).[80]

Freyberg assumed command as the balance of his forces were arriving and moving to assembly areas, leaving him no small task to organize his command, prepare his plans and distribute capabilities. Complicating his task was his total lack of a headquarters and an abundance of non-essential personnel and units stranded after their escape from Greece.

Freyberg and his 2nd NZ Division were evacuated from Greece and landed on Crete largely by accident. Gen Freyberg went ashore to arrange transport for his Division to Alexandria, while ashore Freyberg met with Gen Wavell. At this meeting, Gen Wavell presented the command to Gen Freyberg, replacing Gen Weston, at the direction of Churchill himself.[81] Prior to the conclusion of his meeting Freyberg arranged to have all excess service and support personnel removed from the island, totaling approximately 15,000 personnel.[82]

Culling the excess personnel would have been more efficient and less quarrelsome if Freyberg had a proper staff. The CreForce staff under Gen Weston also represented the MNBDO staff. When Freyberg replaced him, Weston took his staff back to the MNBDO.[83] Rather than order their return Freyberg chose not to do so. To further complicate the issue Freyberg's own staff, the 2nd NZ Divisional staff, had sailed for Cairo hours earlier with his 6th NZ Brigade, and the 6th Australian Division headquarters had sailed the day prior. That left Freyberg as the commander of CreForce alone except for an aide, some signalers and a car.[84]

While assembling the CreForce staff, Freyberg set to work organizing the Cretan Defense and distributing the limited heavy weapons systems. It appears that Gen Weston had established a process and temporary camps to accomplish this task. Shore authorities met units disembarking at Suda Bay, collected their heavy weapons and dispersed the units to a series of camps along the Cretan coast.[85] When units left the camps to move to their sectors, they returned to the quays to claim their weapons only to find they had been redistributed.[86]

INTELLIGENCE

In so far as the Allies were challenged by personnel, equipment, and airpower, they held a momentous advantage when it came to intelligence. Not only did the SOE and SIS have extensive human intelligence collection networks within the Axis, but they had cracked the German communication codes. A secret decoding establishment at Bletchley Park, in England, was able to intercept and decode Germany's most secret transmissions. It is through this establishment, known as Ultra, which the Allies first learned of Operation Mercury.

Through Ultra, the Allies learned: the date of the invasion, the roles and objectives of the XI *Fliegerkorps*, the locations and movement tables of units to Greek bases, of the postponement of the operation until 20 May 1941.[87] If the Allies knew so much about the impending invasion, then the question must be asked, why were they so unprepared and ineffective? Only Gen Freyberg can answer that question.

Freyberg first learned about Ultra after he became commander of CreForce.[88] Once in command, Ultra transcripts pertaining to the invasion of Crete came directly to him. They detailed the operational specifics of the German invasion from times, to landing zones and objectives. So, why did he continue to orient his defenses on the beaches rather than the drop zones?

First, "super secret" intelligence such as Ultra could not be revealed directly or indirectly, otherwise the Germans may suspect their system to be compromised and change it, therefore drying up the well. Likewise, Freyberg was not able to discuss where and how he received the intelligence in order to properly plan for it.

Second, Ultra transcripts also warned of German intentions to support the airborne invasion with an amphibious landing. As a diligent commander, Freyberg likely required his staff to conduct a staff estimate concerning the probable strength the Germans could muster for an amphibious assault. Without understanding the airborne capability of the *Luftwaffe* and the enormity of the airborne assault, as only Ultra could describe, it is likely the staff estimates underestimated the size of the airborne assault and overestimated the more familiar amphibious assault. Thus the staffs at CreForce, GHQ Middle East and even in London, albeit unaware of Ultra intelligence, presented an unrealistic amphibious capability – 10,000 troops by sea.[89]

Third, in safeguarding the secret of Ultra, Freyberg was prohibited from sharing his puzzle. As he likely saw it, CreForce faced an airborne assault to seize key terrain – a harbor – and facilitate the landing of 10,000 troops. The airborne concept was so new it is hardly likely that Freyberg could have predicted the Germans could drop the balance of a division.[90] Yet, the Ultra intercepts outlined a divisional airborne assault. On two occasions prior to the assault, paper orders were captured that confirmed the predictions.[91]

In the end, the windfall of intelligence decoded at Bletchley Park could have helped win the Battle of Crete. However, Freyberg continued to organize and orient his defenses around landing beaches and approaches from the sea and Ultra's secrets had very little positive impact on the Allied defenses.

THE DEFENSE

Freyberg adopted Weston's defensive plan (APPENDIX H), which in turn relied on Tidbury's initial assessment. The plan outlined five sectors and identified headquarters and forces for each. The most eastern sector, dominated by the largest city and accessible via landing beaches, a harbor, and a large airport was designated Heraklion Sector (APPENDIX M). Brigadier B.H. Chappel commanded Heraklion. Freyberg considered Heraklion an independent command provided Chappel a heavily reinforced brigade (APPENDIX R). To Heraklion's west was designated the Retimo Sector (APPENDIX N) commanded by Brigadier George Vasey. Retimo included the town of Retimo, the Retimo airport, and Georgeoupolis Beach. Vasey was allocated an under strength brigade to operate his defense (APPENDIX R). Weston and the MNDBO were responsible for the port at Suda Bay (APPENDIX I) and the air defense and coastal defense guns defending the port. Weston retained the MNBDO and was responsible for the 15,000 service and support personnel in his sector but lacked any significant offensive capability (APPENDIX P).

Should Suda Bay be threatened, Weston would have to look west to Canea (APPENDIX K) and Brigadier Edward Puttick, Freyberg's successor at 2nd NZ Division. Canea was comprised of the most permissive terrain and was accessible via large landing beaches. As such, Freyberg allowed Puttick to retain command and control of the balance of 2nd NZ Division (APPENDIX Q). To Puttick's west lay Maleme Sector (APPENDIX L) and the remainder of the

NZ Division, CreForce's most western flank, commanded by Brigadier James Hargest (APPENDIX Q).

As mentioned above, the command relationship shared by Gen Puttick and his Brigadiers likely had a significant impact on CreForce's effectiveness. The CreForce headquarters was located in Suda, central to the four western sectors. By design, Freyberg intended each of the sector commanders to coordinate through him. Weston in Suda and Chappel in Heraklion did. However, Putticks 2nd NZ Division complicated the relationship between CreForce, Canea, Retimo and Maleme. The 2nd NZ Division, and Puttick, often attempted to direct the actions in both Maleme and Retimo because those Brigades and their commanders habitually belonged to the division. On two occasions, Hargest's counter-attacks failed because Puttick limited the units he could use. Similarly, in Retimo, rather than using his available forces at Georgeoupolis to reinforce his forces in Retimo, Puttick directed Vasey to reinforce the Canea sector. Rather than directing and synchronizing five independent sectors in one synchronized effort, Freyberg's command and control was handicapped by an unnecessary command and control echelon.

While CreForce did suffer severe equipment deficiencies - crew served weapons, artillery, and motorized transport – the most significant was communication equipment.[92] Not only were the sectors unable to communicate via "wireless," but there was not a reliable wire network.[93] Units communicated through runners to the brigades. The brigades' most reliable communication to CreForce was either runner or tactical wire. Depending on either was precarious, as the bombs of the *Luftwaffe* tended to destroy wire communications and was equally punishing to vehicles or personnel in the open. Hargest, a Sector Commander, communicated to Puttick and Freyberg through the Cretan phone system.[74] Even though Freyberg identified a lack of communications infrastructure early in his command, not one senior commander from CreForce to Cairo thought to request communication equipment. A single airplane load of equipment, in this case, may have swayed the outcome of Crete.

THE RESULTS

From 14 May through 19 May 1941 the *Luftwaffe* mercilessly bombed the landing zones and defenses of Crete. On 20 May 1941 the German glider and airborne assault proceeded under heavy air cover dropping 10,000 *Fallschirmjäger* into and behind CreForce's ill-sited defenses. CreForce's defensive architecture oriented the coastal defense guns, the howitzers and field guns seaward. Likewise, the trenches pillboxes and redoubts protecting the beaches were positioned in the middle of the German landing zones predicted by Gen Tidbury more than six months before. Consequently, the infantry were unable to benefit from indirect fires. In fact, Freyberg's decision to downplay an airborne assault likely thickened the fog of war and increased the Allied confusion. Instead of the enemy crawling up the beaches, they were landing amongst the defensive positions (APPENDICES I,J,K,L,M and N).

The Germans landing in and around the defensive positions were easy prey, but confused the situation. Due to poor communications, units in the defense were unable to determine if the units to their left and right were still intact. Commanders sent out parties to search out the enemy, but they did so cautiously. The slowness to react aided the decimated Germans, allowing them to consolidate, reorganize and proceed *in ordnung*.

By nightfall only 6,000 *Fallschirmjäger* remained. Unwittingly, the Allies had nearly defeated the Germans on day one. The heavy losses taken by the Germans in the first wave had denied them their initial objectives, but they controlled the perimeter of the Maleme airfield by virtue of Allied miscommunication and confusion. The counterattack German commanders feared would defeat them never materialized. Instead, Freyberg held back, waiting to defeat the amphibious assault he still believed would come. This combined with the time taken to understand the situation and mount a counterattack bought the Germans time to land the 5th *Gebirgs Division* at the Maleme airfield (APPENDIX W).

From 21 May until the evacuation of the Allied force starting on 29 May, the battle between the Allies (30,000 Allies and 10,000 Greeks) and the German XI *Fliegerkorps* (18,000) raged.[96] The ever-present Luftwaffe, growing supply shortages and ritualistic sacrifices of recently hard won ground plagued the Allies. In turn, the Germans continued to sustain heavy losses, but pressed forward, buoyed by the effectiveness of the *Luftwaffe*, resolute leadership and unity of command. On 1 Jun 1941 the final Allied transport departed Crete leaving some 5,000 Allied personnel behind.[97] The Battle for Crete was lost.

CONCLUSION

The Allies failed to clearly define, articulate and implement the strategic objectives of their entry into Greece. As a result, subordinate commanders were unable or unwilling to create the operational level unity of command that would allow them to synchronize their efforts to achieve the national objectives. Instead, responsible commanders attempted to tackle their individual situation as they believed it applied to the nefarious strategic objectives.

Separately, no single command was able to collect, organize and synchronize the combat power and resources necessary to achieve the overall objective. Consequently, the tactical commander, Freyberg, was presented a situation riddled with complexities, which he had no ability to control. Due to strategic disagreements, and operational self-interest General Freyberg was charged with achieving national objectives without the resources required. Thus his utilization and synchronization of the elements of combat power were misplaced and therefore unable to produce victory.

However, had General Freyberg planned and organized his meager resources around the intelligence he was provided, the outcome of the Battle of Crete would have been reversed. CreForce outnumbered their attackers, had the benefit of interior lines, nearly perfect intelligence, and sufficient personnel and equipment to defeat a much larger force than the Germans could have presented. Had the defense been oriented against denying an airborne assault, the Allied soldiers would have received the victory they deserved.

APPENDIX A: Maps of Crete

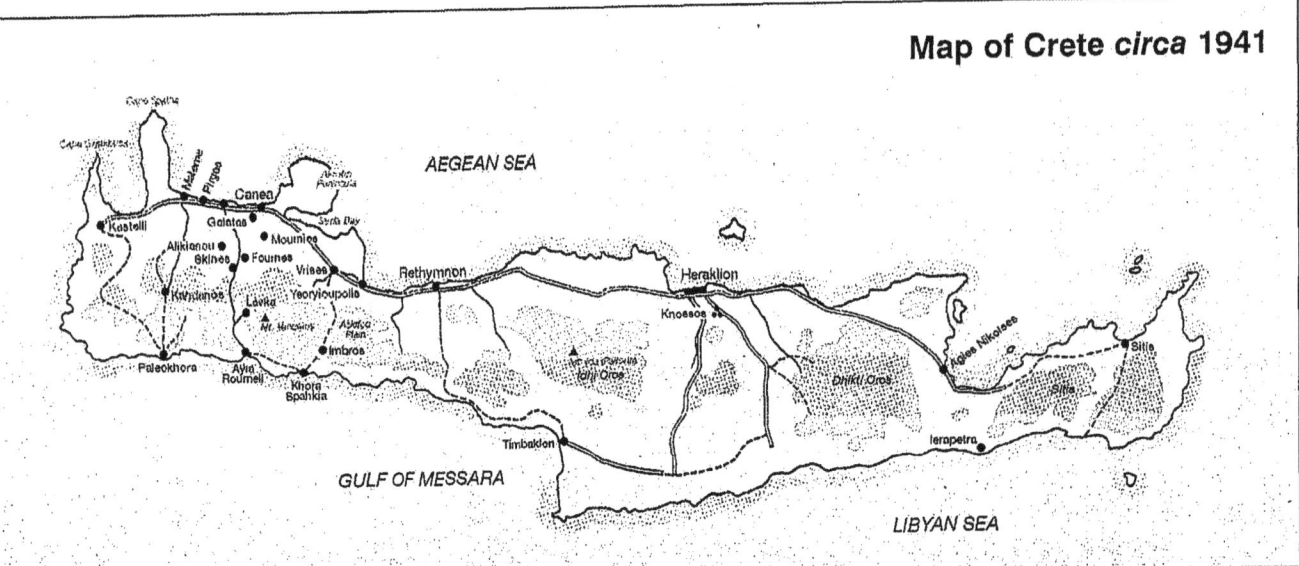

Source: *Battle of Crete*, George Forty, pg 12

Source: *Battle of Crete*, Albert Palazzo, pg 13

APPENDIX B: Crete and the Mediterranean

EASTERN MEDITERRANEAN

Source: *Crete*, D.M. Davin, cover

APPENDIX C: Reinforcements Intercepted

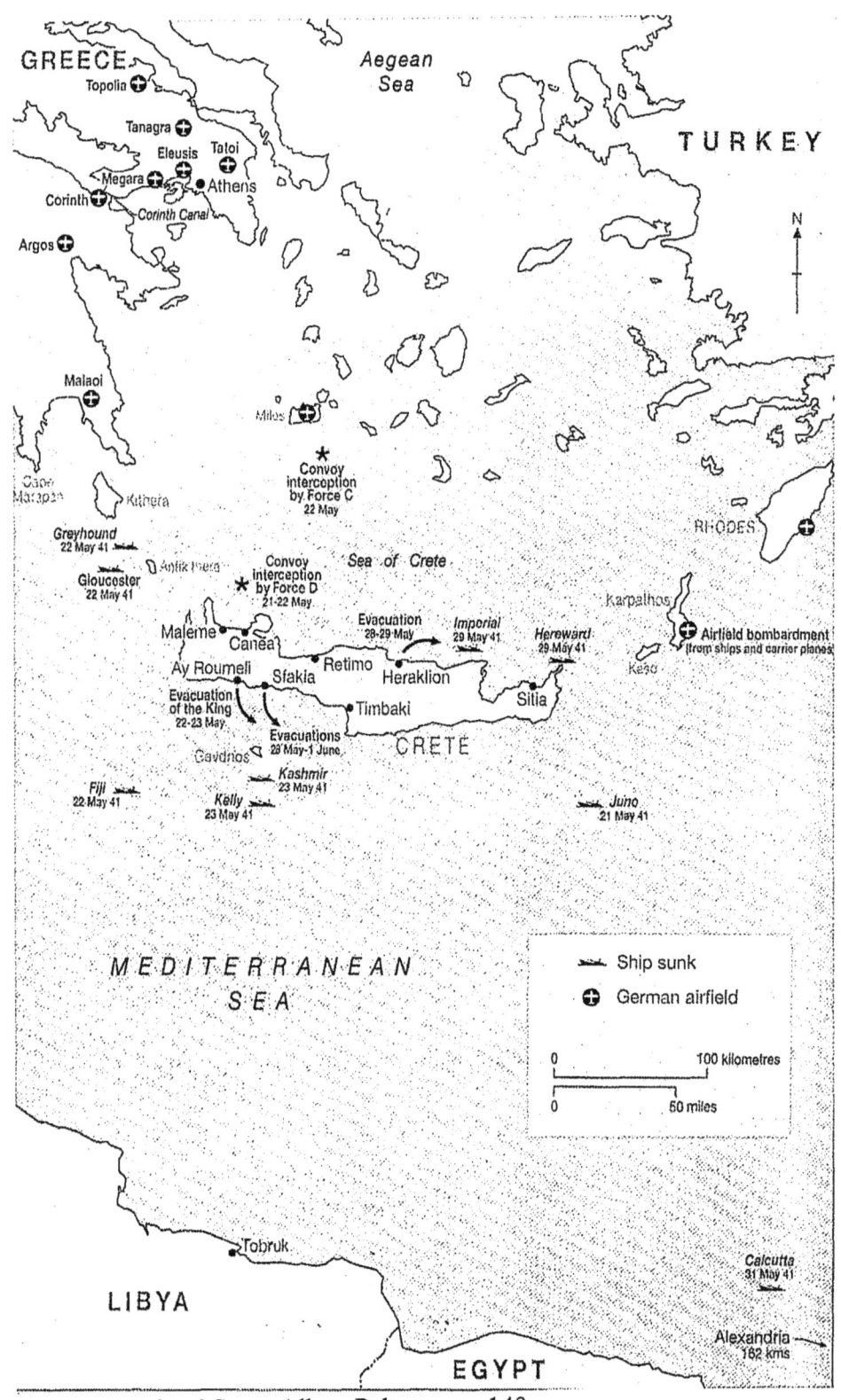

Source: *Battle of Crete*, Albert Palazzo, pg 149

APPENDIX D: Air Bases in the Eastern Mediterranean

Source: *Battle of Crete*, Albert Palazzo, pg 156

APPENDIX E: Aircraft Ranges

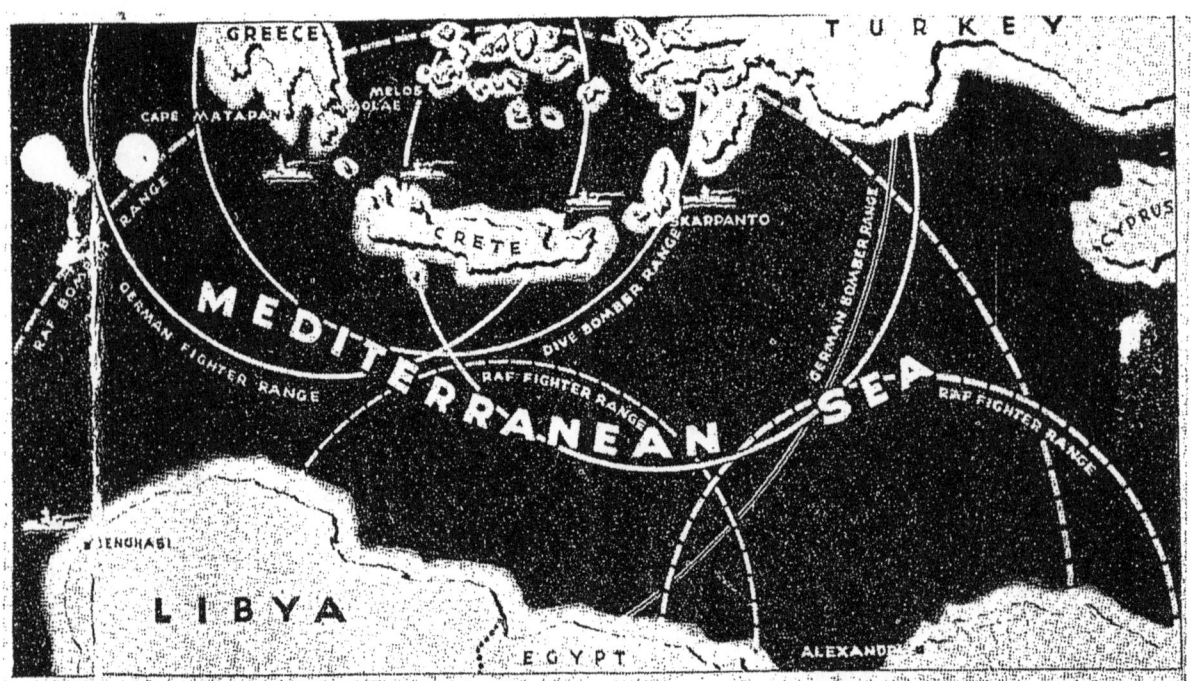

Source: *Battle for Crete*, Army Board, pg 25

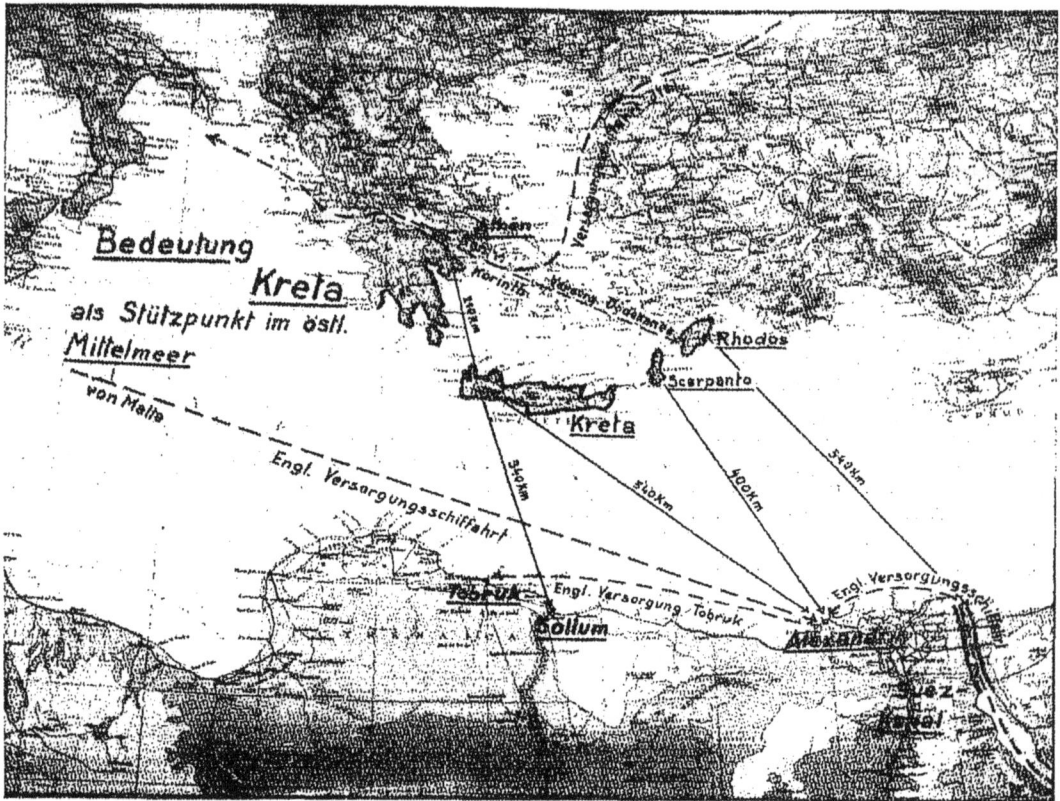

Source: *Battle of Crete*, Albert Palazzo, pg 12

APPENDIX F: Allied Chain of Command

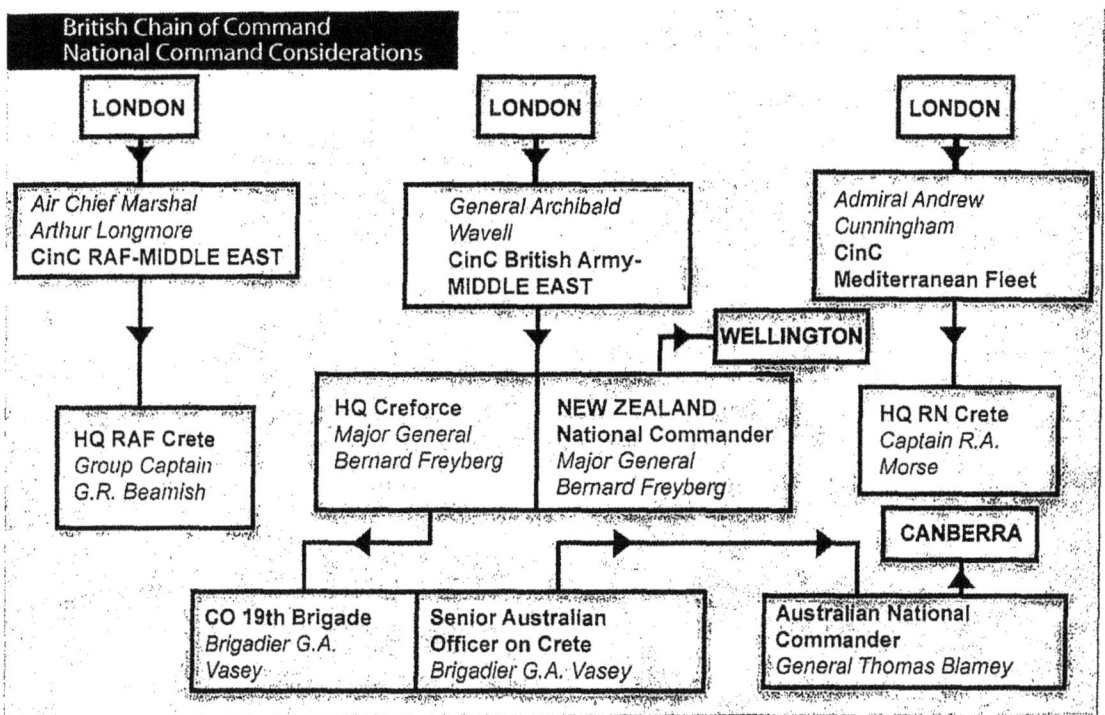

Source: *Battle of Crete*, Albert Palazzo, pg 24

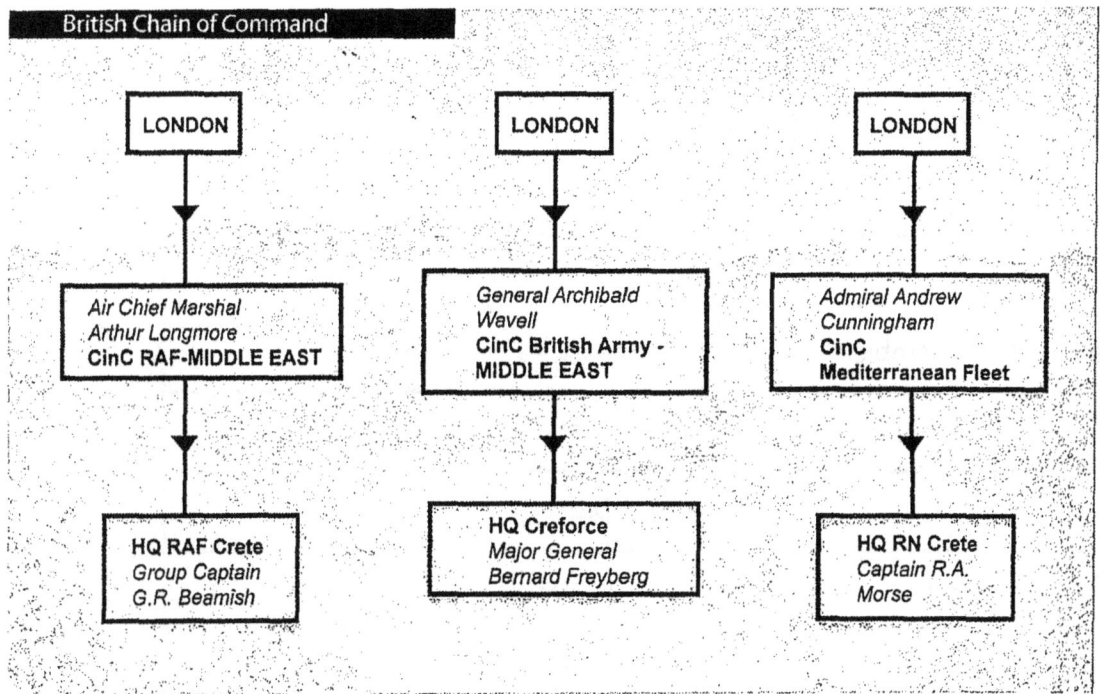

Source: *Battle of Crete*, Albert Palazzo, pg 24

APPENDIX G: German Chain of Command and CreForce Commanders

German Chain of Command

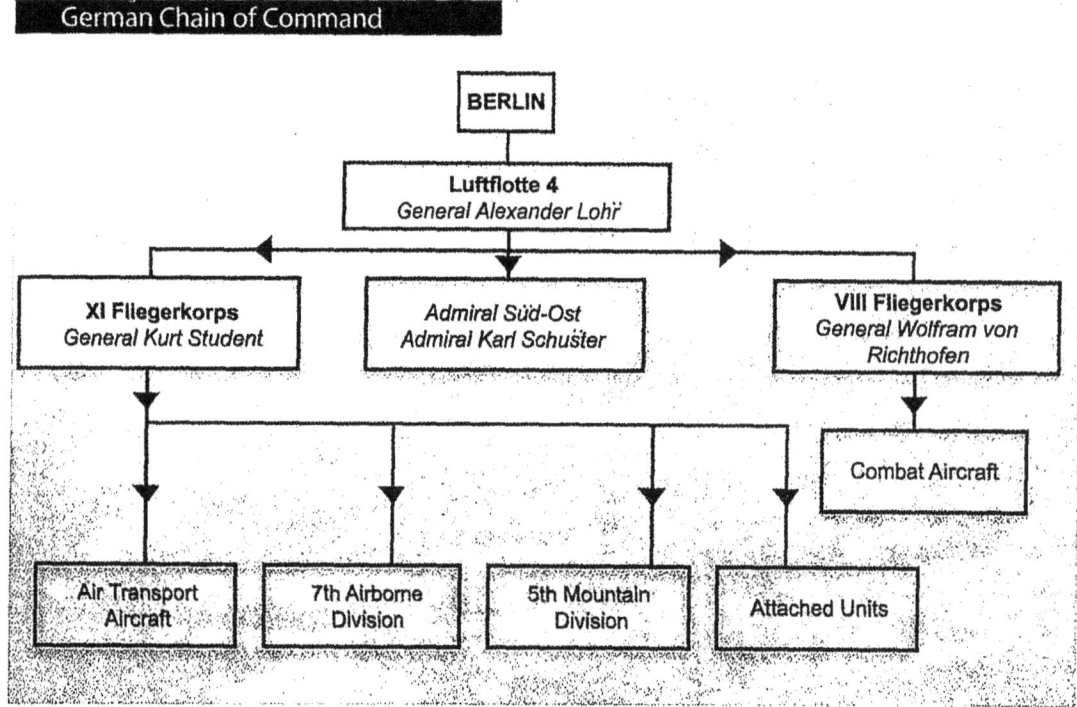

Source: Battle of Crete, Albert Palazzo, pg 23

British Commanders on Crete

Commanders	Duration of Appointment
Brigadier O. H. Tidbury	November 1940 – 9 January 1941
Major-General M. D. Gambier-Parry	9 January – 7 February 1941
Lieutenant-Colonel C. H. Mather	7 February – 19 February 1941
Brigadier A. Galloway	19 February – 9 March 1941
Brigadier B. H. Chappel	20 March – 22 April 1941
Major-General E. C. Weston	22 April – 30 April 1941
Major-General B. C. Freyberg	30 April – 30 May 1941

Source: Battle of Crete, Albert Palazzo, pg 14

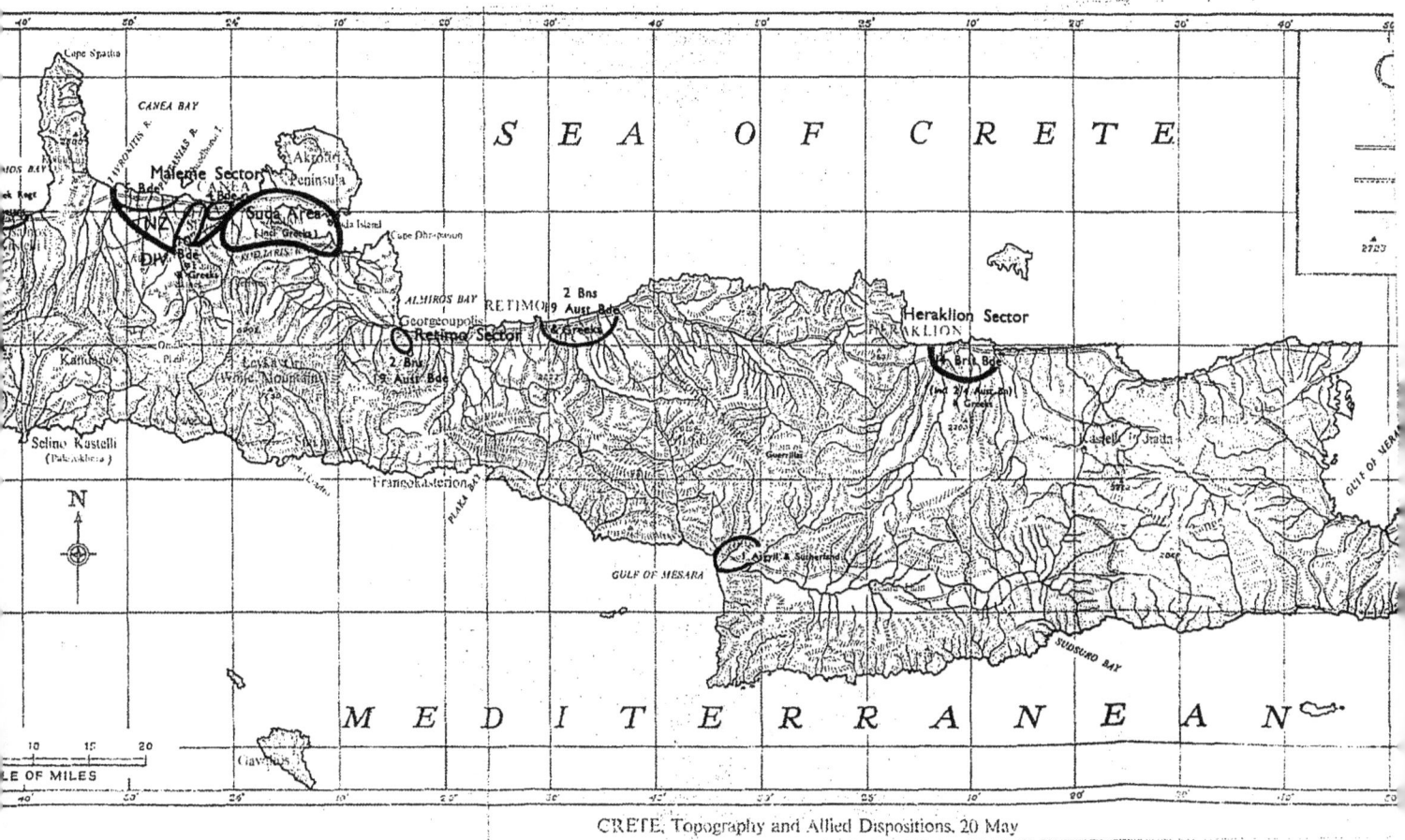

CRETE. Topography and Allied Dispositions, 20 May

APPENDIX I: Suda Sector and Fixed Defenses

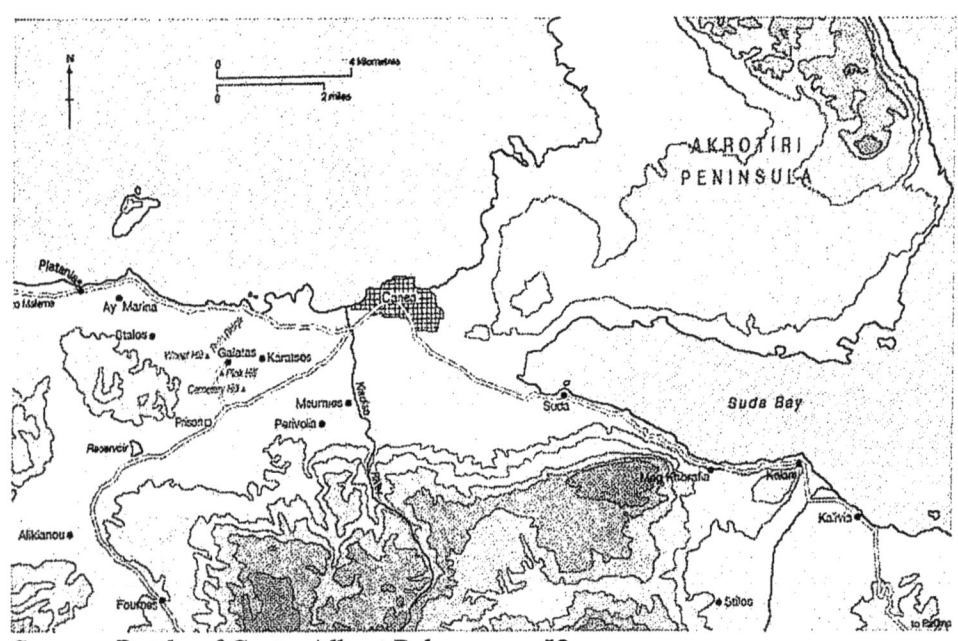

Source: *Battle of Crete*, Albert Palazzo, pg 52

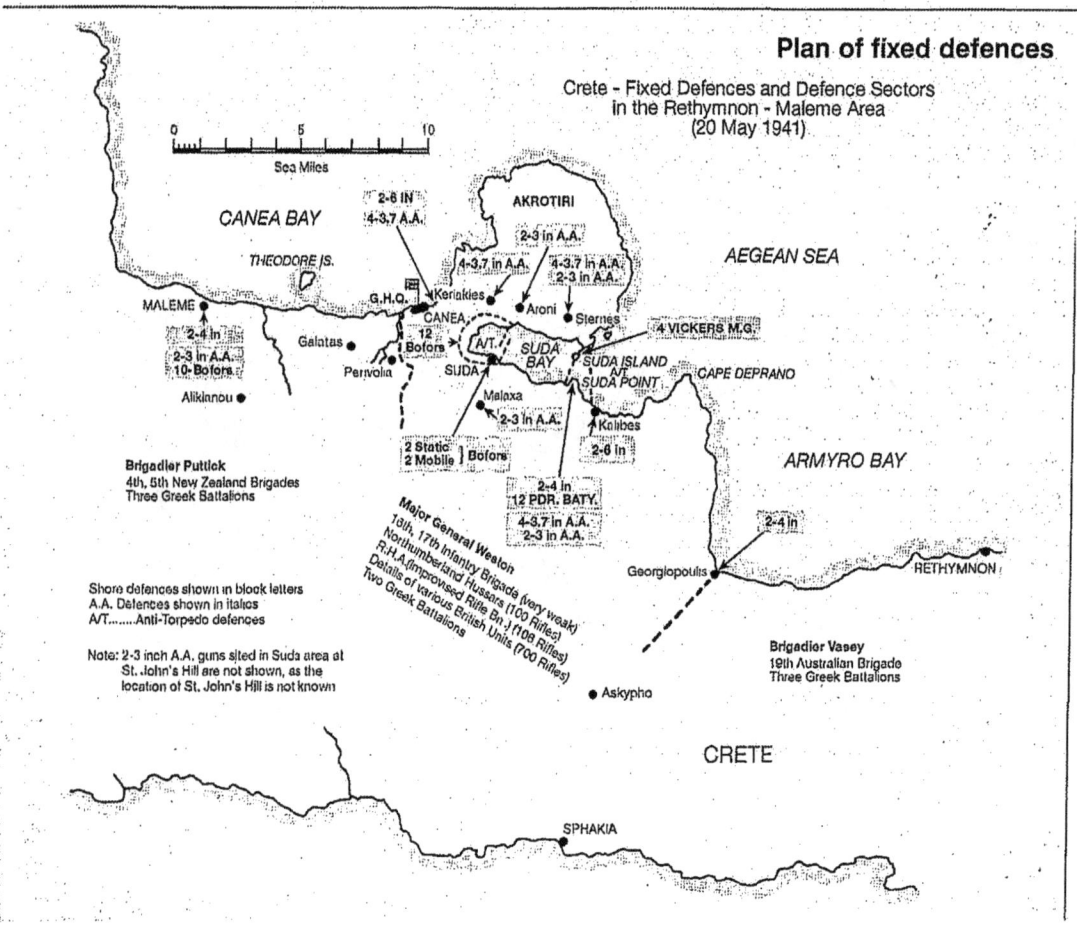

Source: *Battle of Crete*, George Forty, pg 27

APPENDIX J: Suda and Canea Sectors

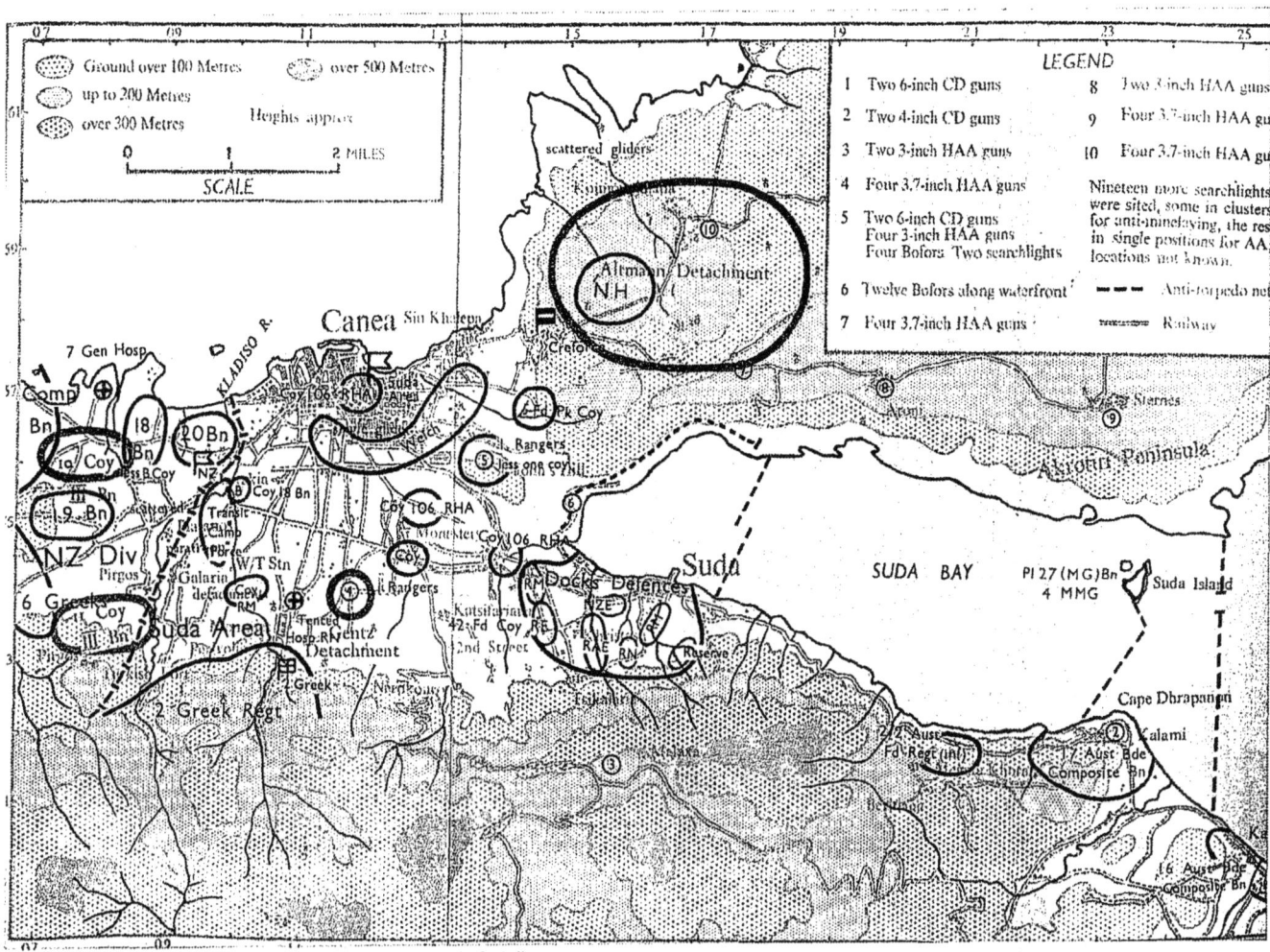

Source: *Crete*, D.M. Davin, pg 151 (tri-fold)

APPENDIX K: Canea Sector

Source: Crete, D.M. Davin, pg 133 (tri-fold)

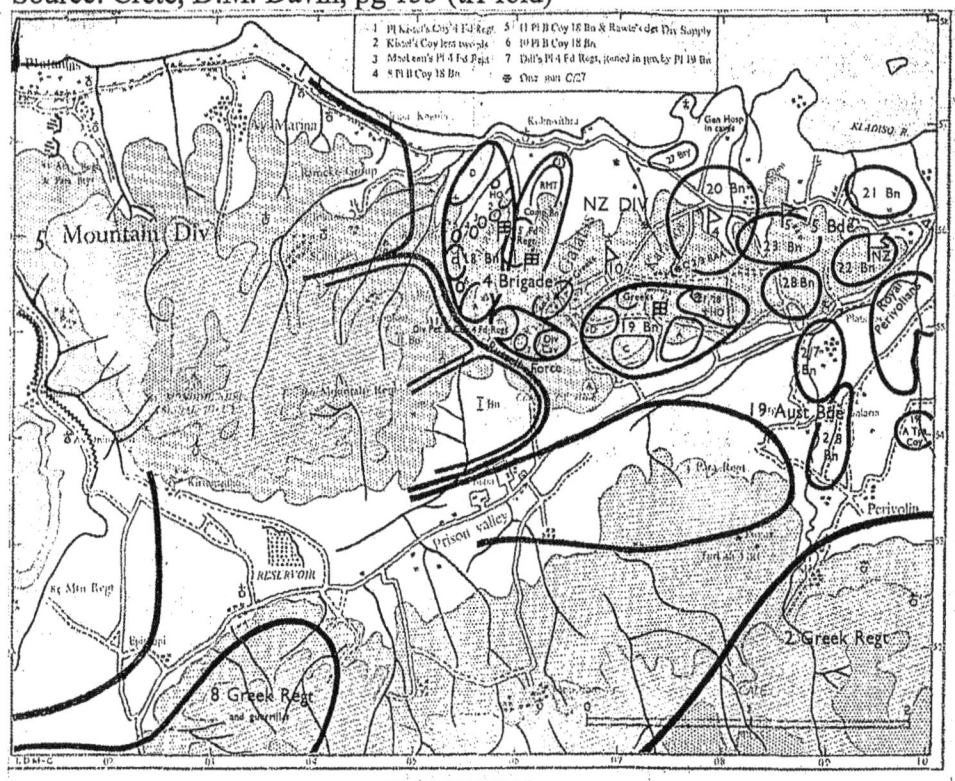

Source: Crete, D.M. Davin, pg 285 (tri-fold)

APPENDIX L: Maleme Sector

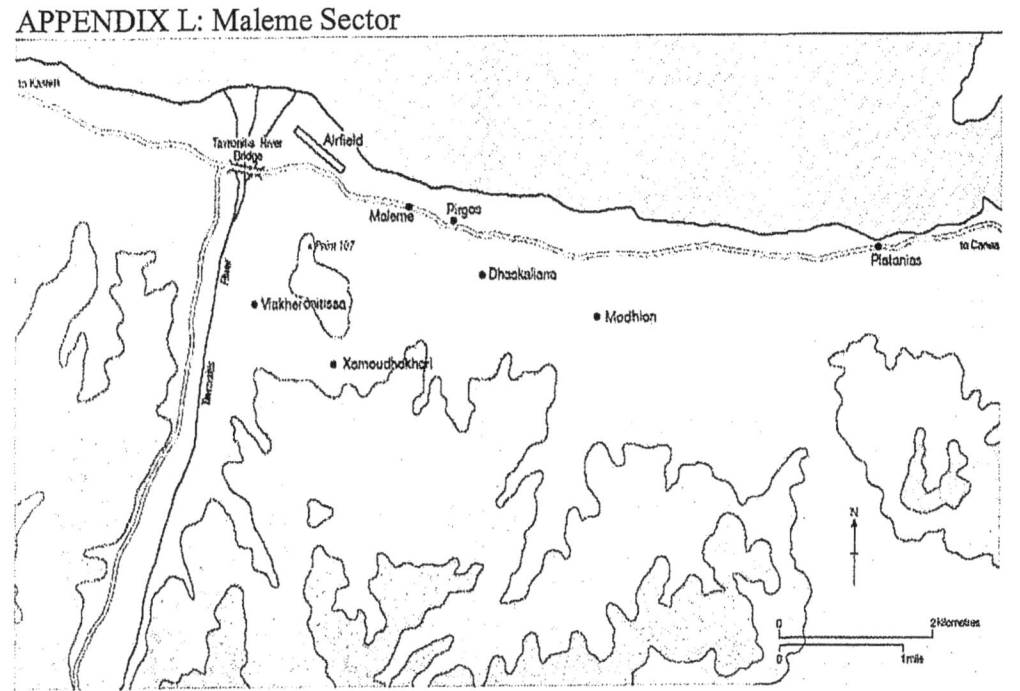

Source: *Battle of Crete*, Albert Palazzo, pg 31

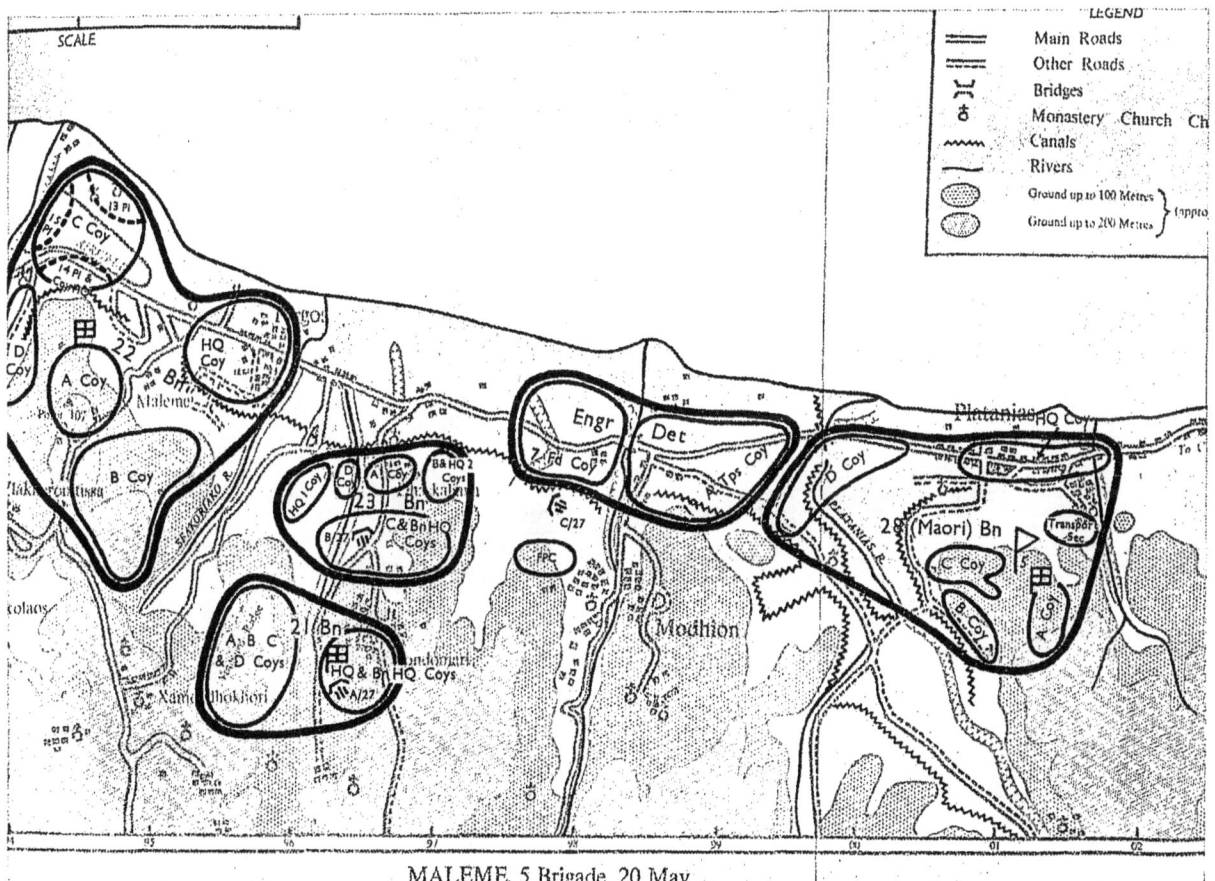

MALEME, 5 Brigade, 20 May

Source: *Crete*, D.M. Davin, pg 97 (tri-fold)

APPENDIX L (cont.): Maleme Sector

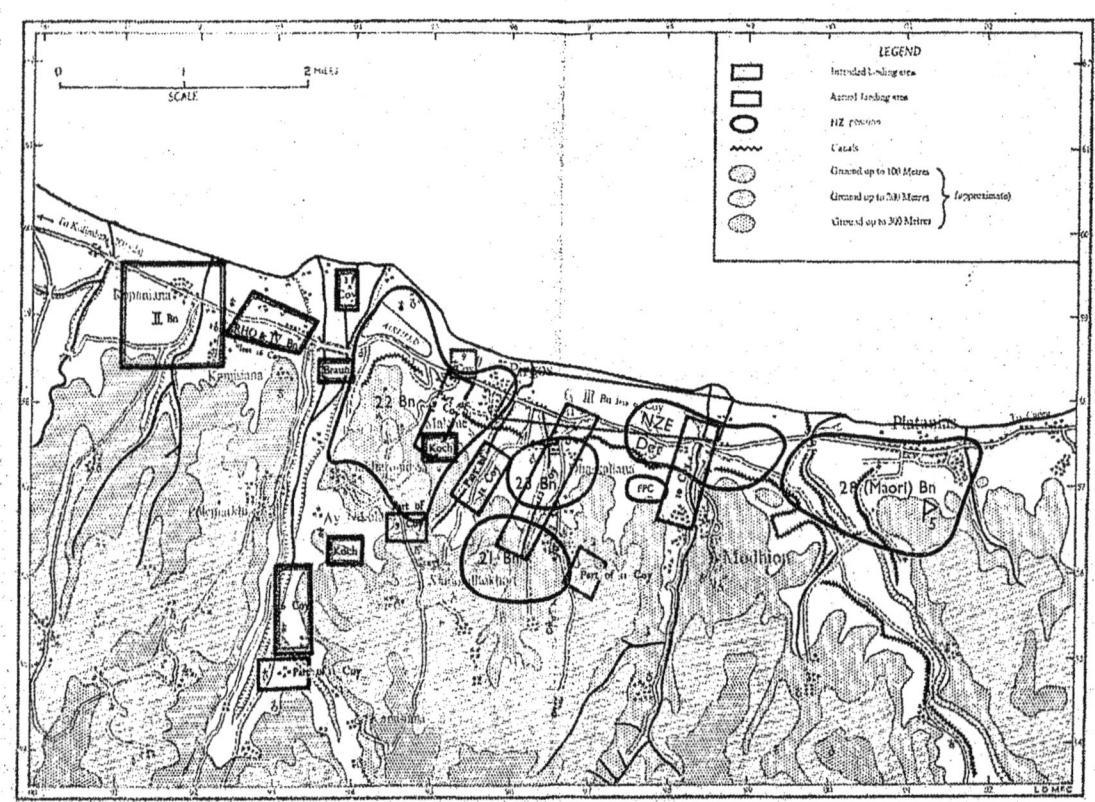

MALEME, Intended and Actual Landing Areas of *Assault Regiment*, 20 May

Source: *Crete*, D.M. Davin, pg 133 (tri-fold)

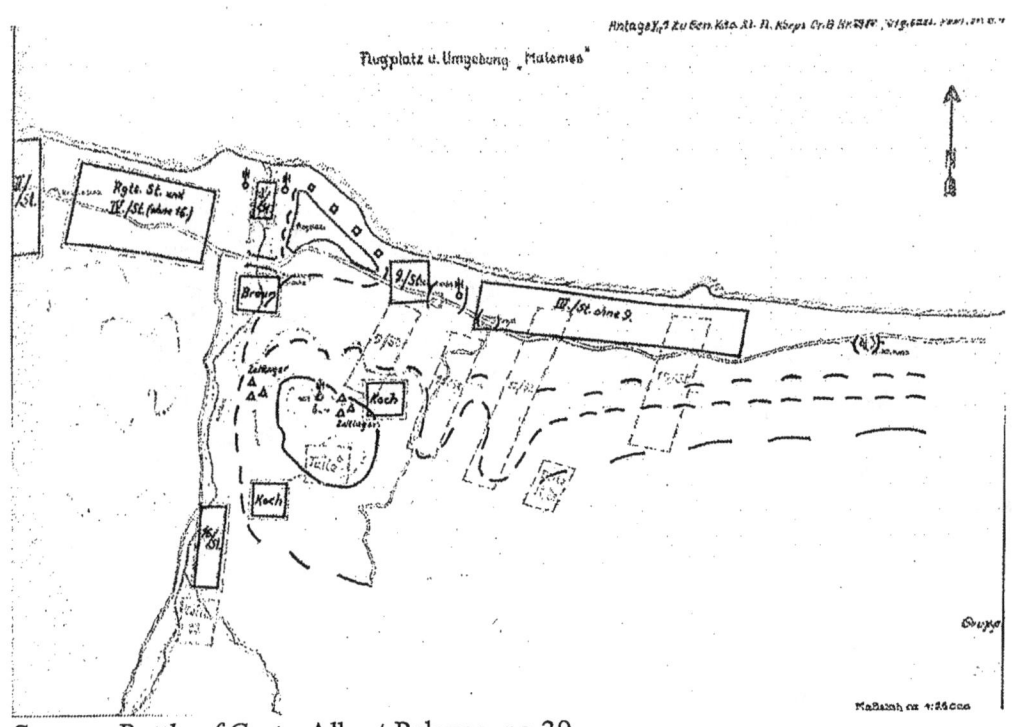

Source: *Battle of Crete*, Albert Palazzo, pg 39

APPENDIX M: Heraklion Sector

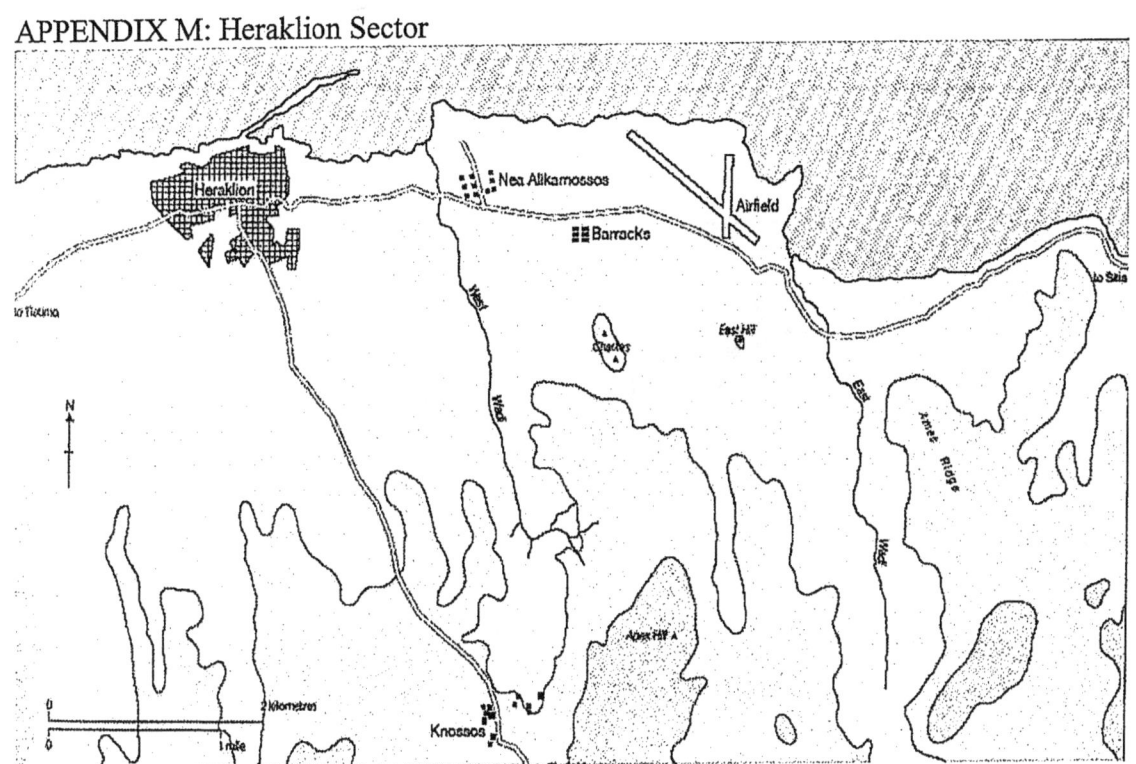

Source: *Battle of Crete*, Albert Palazzo, pg 73

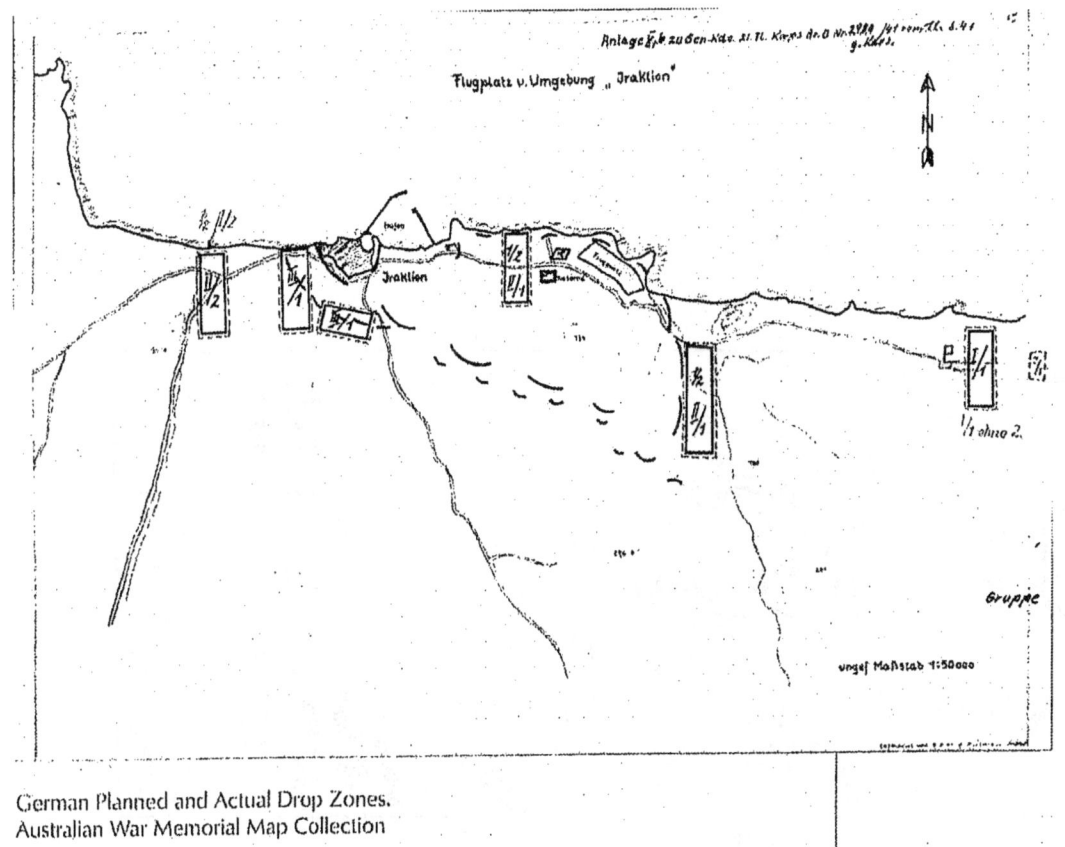

German Planned and Actual Drop Zones.
Australian War Memorial Map Collection

Source: *Battle of Crete*, Albert Palazzo, pg 84

APPENDIX M (cont.) Heraklion Sector

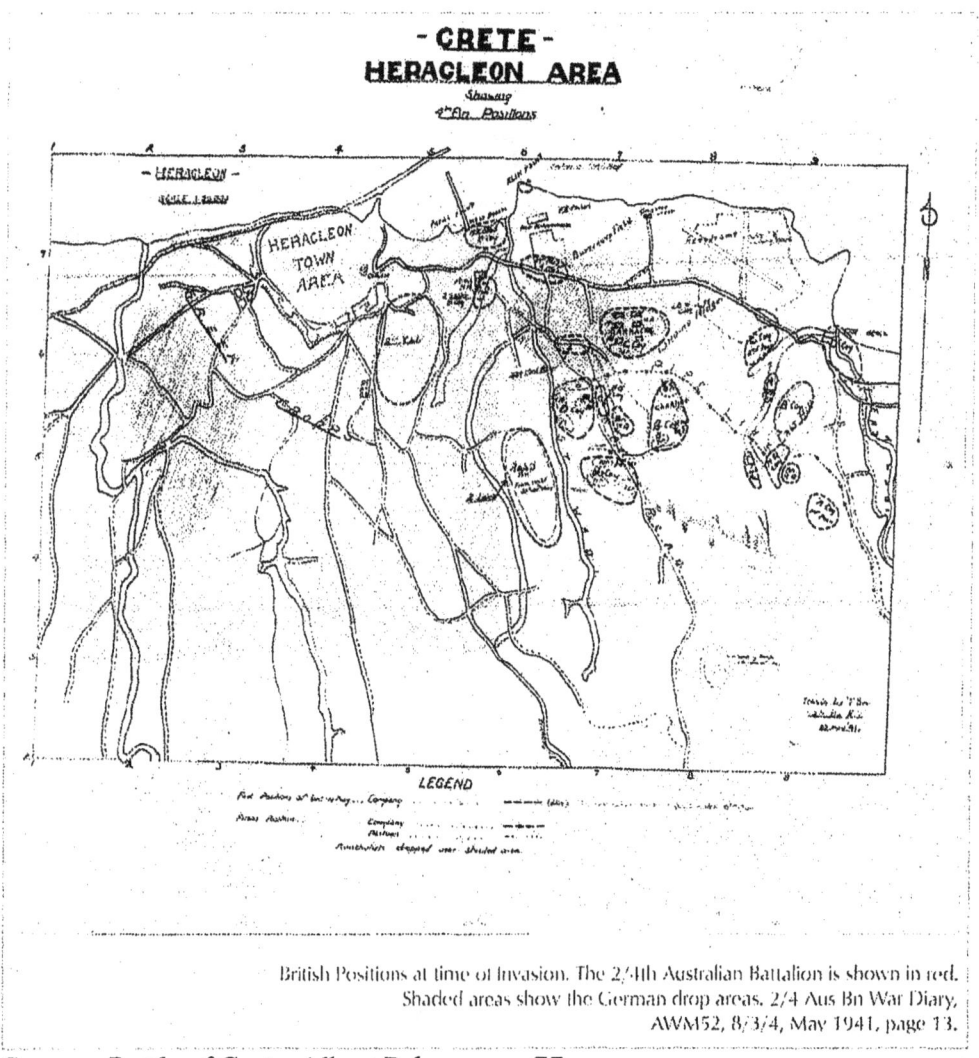

British Positions at time of Invasion. The 2/4th Australian Battalion is shown in red. Shaded areas show the German drop areas. 2/4 Aus Bn War Diary, AWM52, 8/3/4, May 1941, page 13.

Source: *Battle of Crete*, Albert Palazzo, pg 77

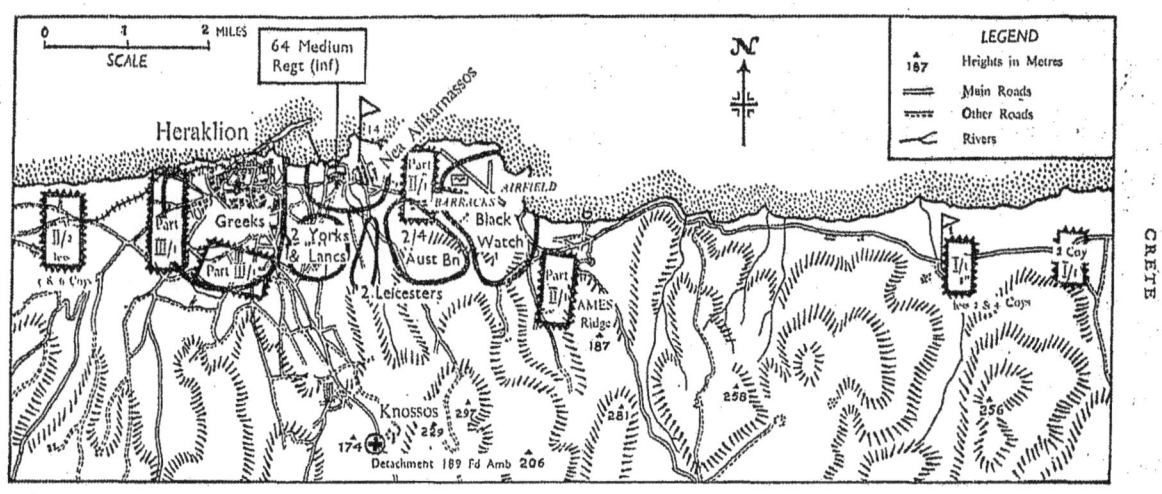

HERAKLION, 20 MAY

Source: *Crete*, D.M. Davin, pg 178

APPENDIX N: Retimo Sector

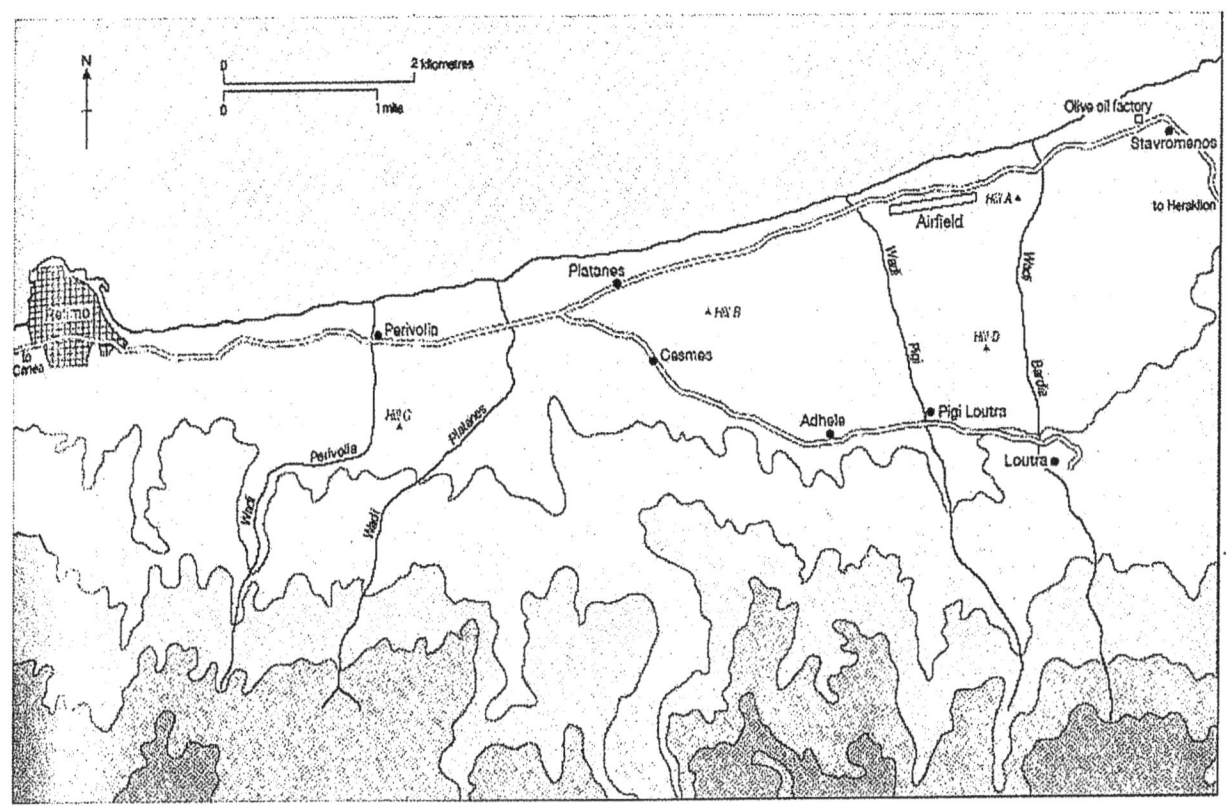

Source: *Battle of Crete*, Albert Palazzo, pg 93

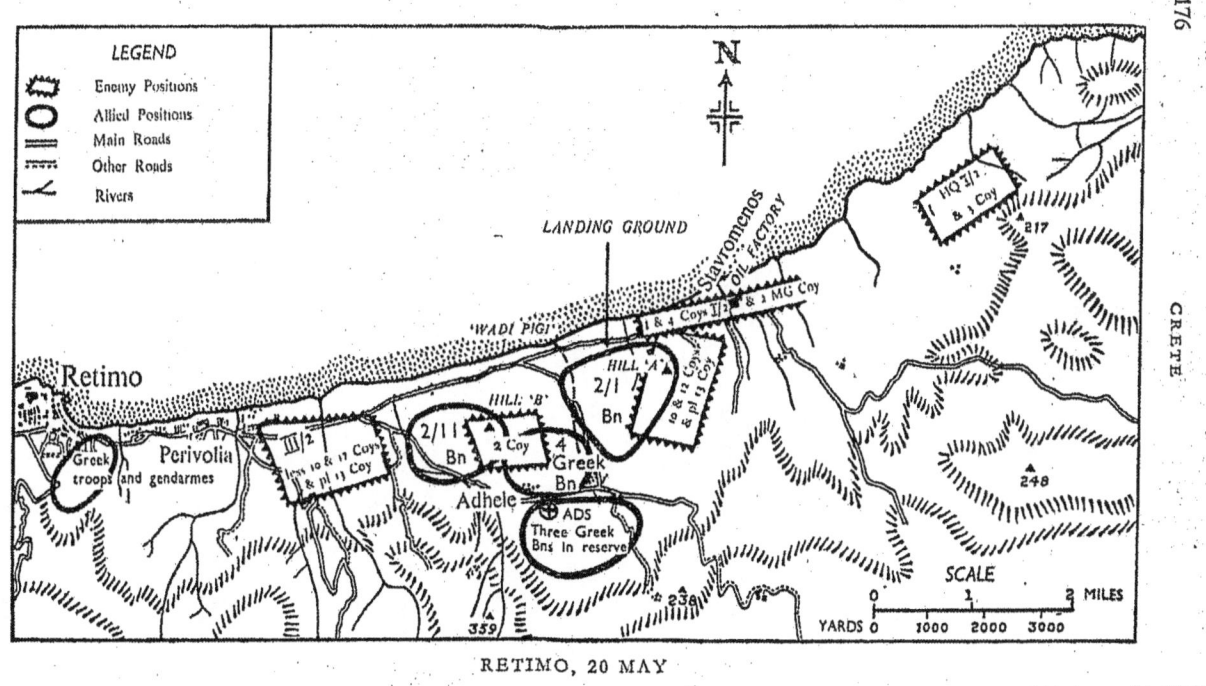

Source: *Crete*, D.M. Davin, pg 176

APPENDIX N (cont.): Retimo Sector

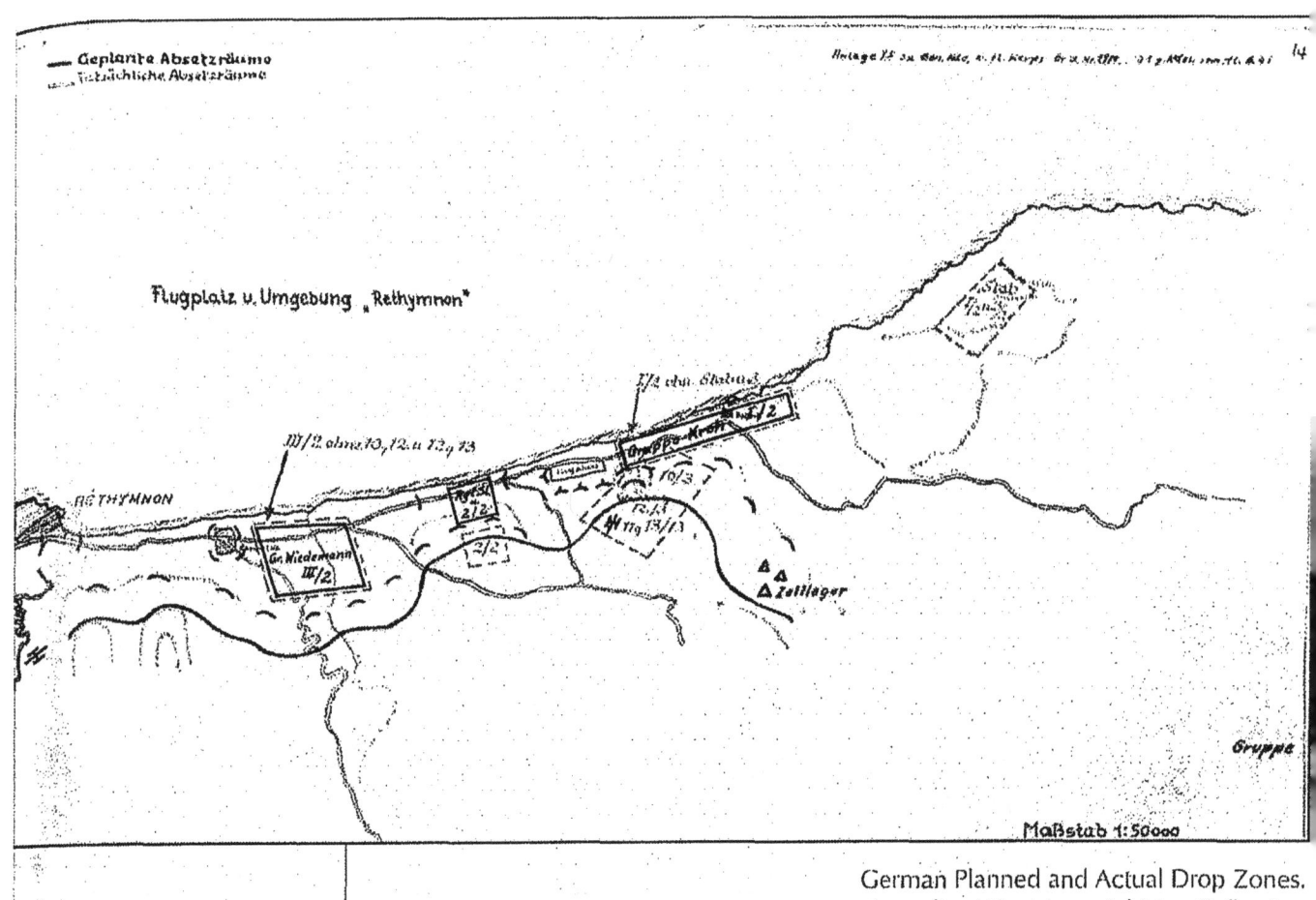

Source: *Battle of Crete*, Albert Palazzo, pg 97

German Planned and Actual Drop Zones.
Australian War Memorial Map Collection

APPENDIX O: CreForce Task Organization

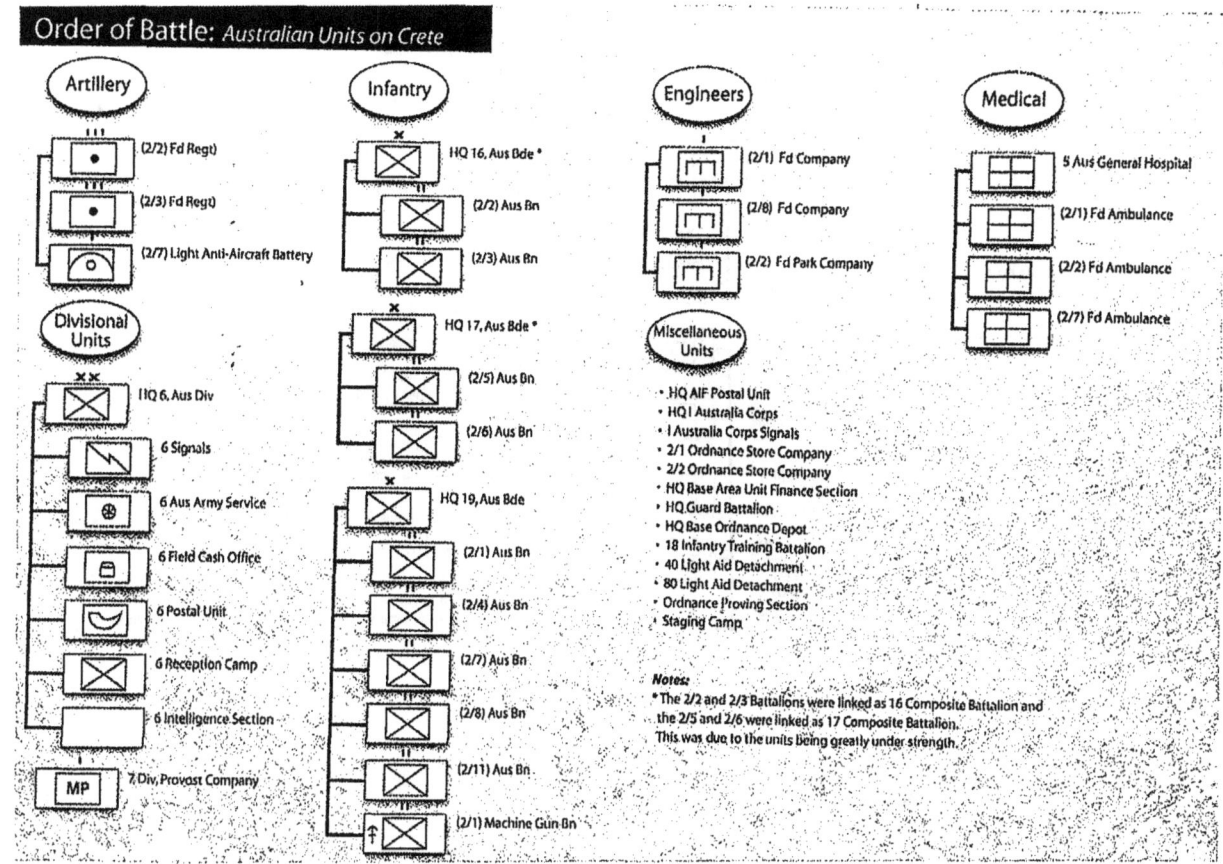

Source: *Battle of Crete*, Albert Palazzo, pg 22

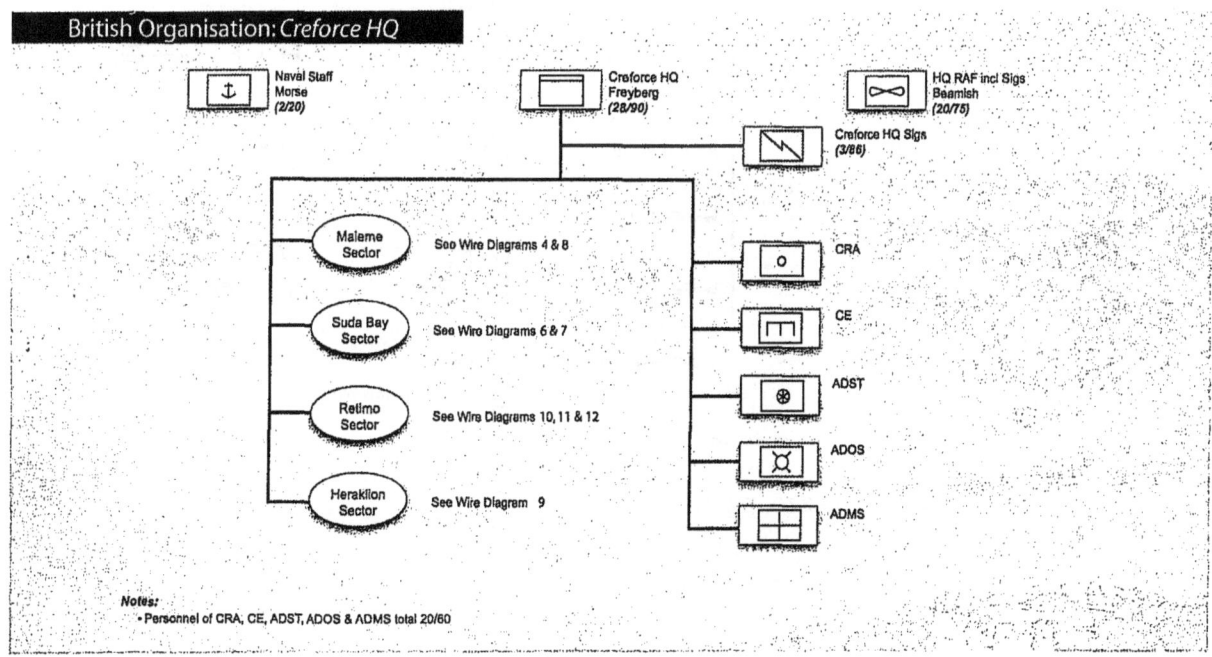

Source: *Battle of Crete*, Albert Palazzo, pg 53

APPENDIX P: Suda Sector Task Organization

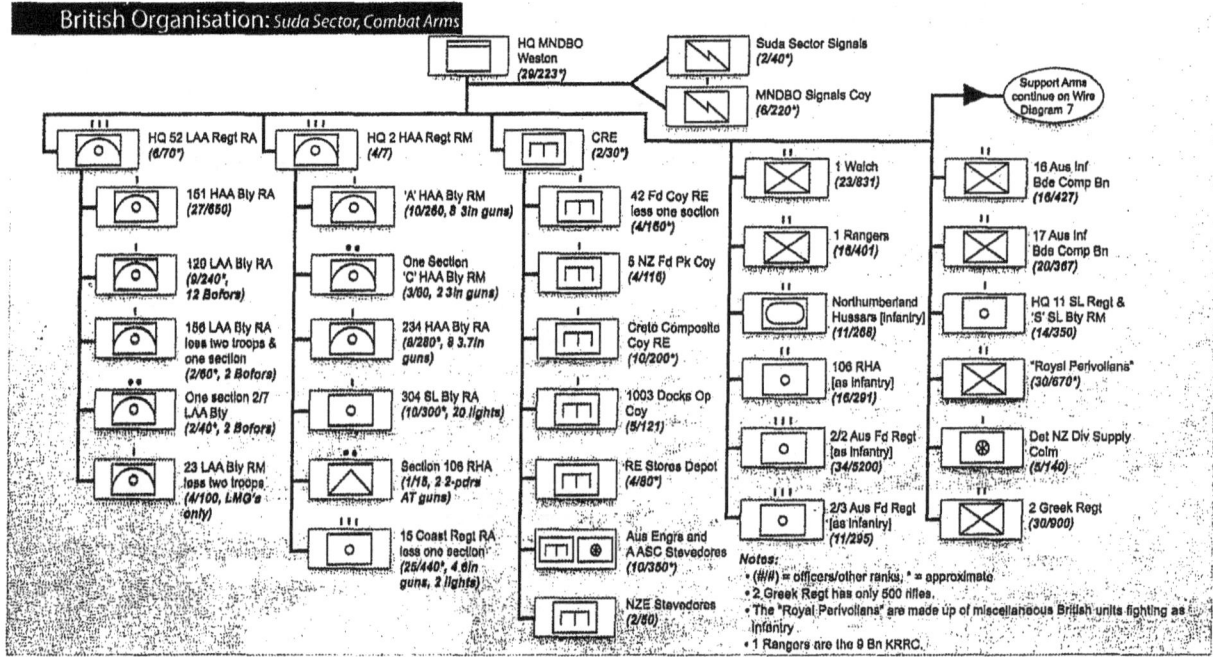

Source: *Battle of Crete*, Albert Palazzo, pg 55

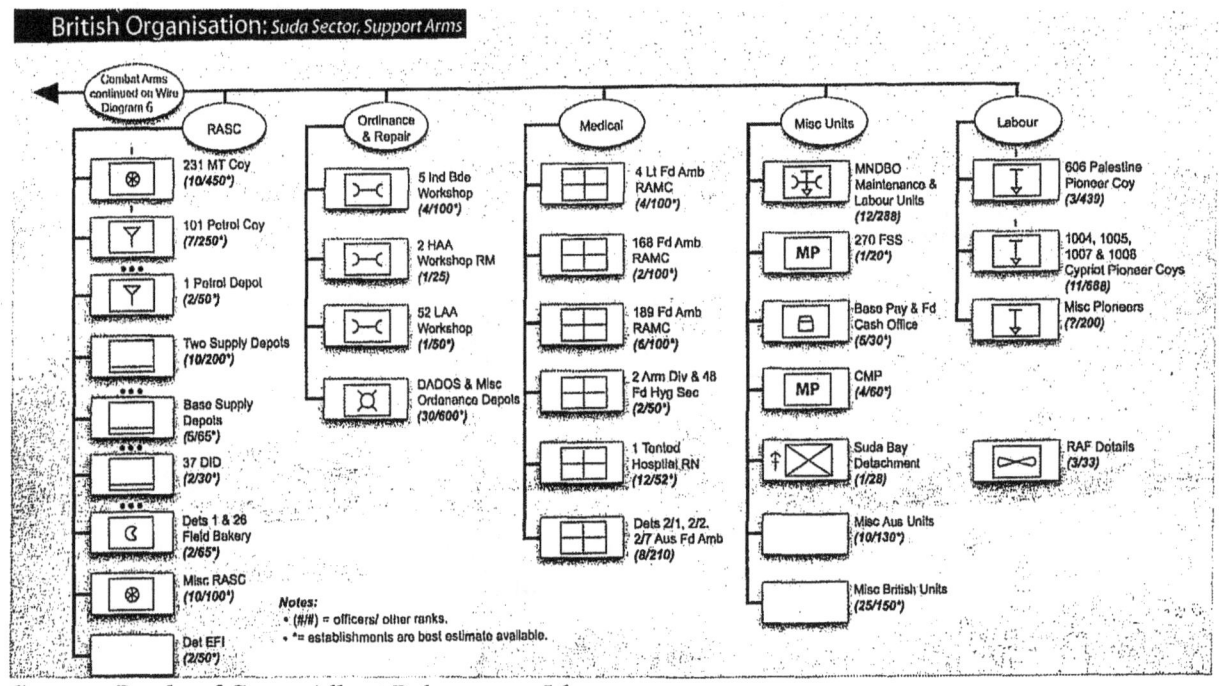

Source: *Battle of Crete*, Albert Palazzo, pg 56

APPENDIX Q: Canea and Maleme Sector Task Organization

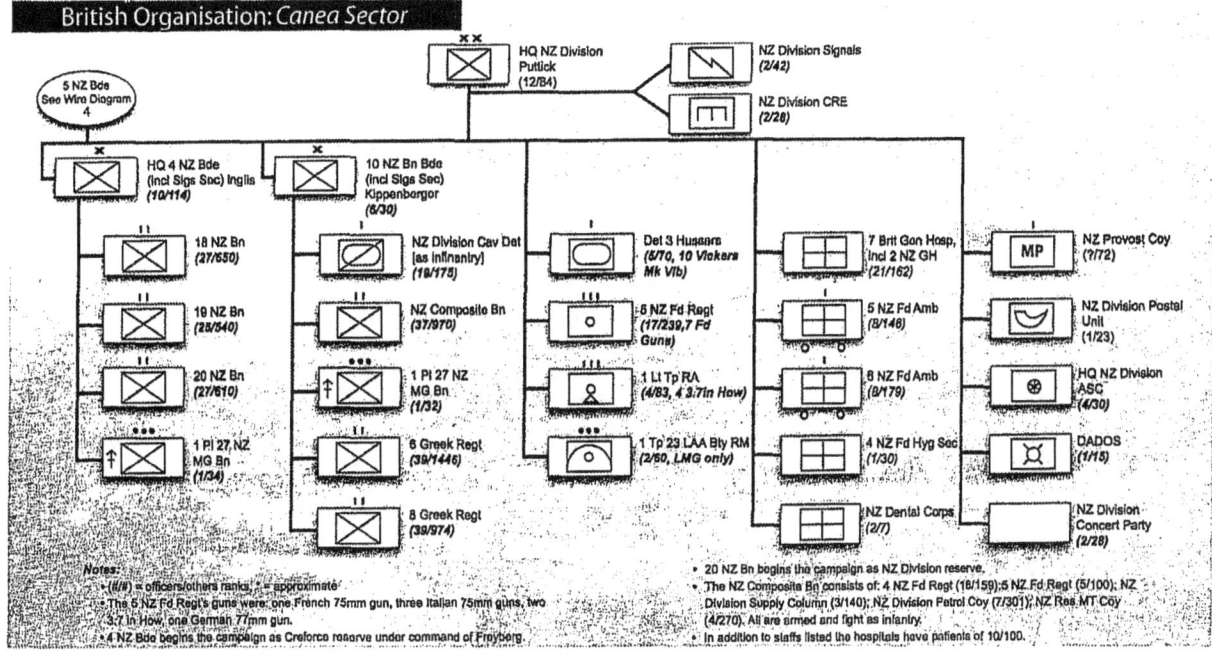

Source: *Battle of Crete*, Albert Palazzo, pg 57

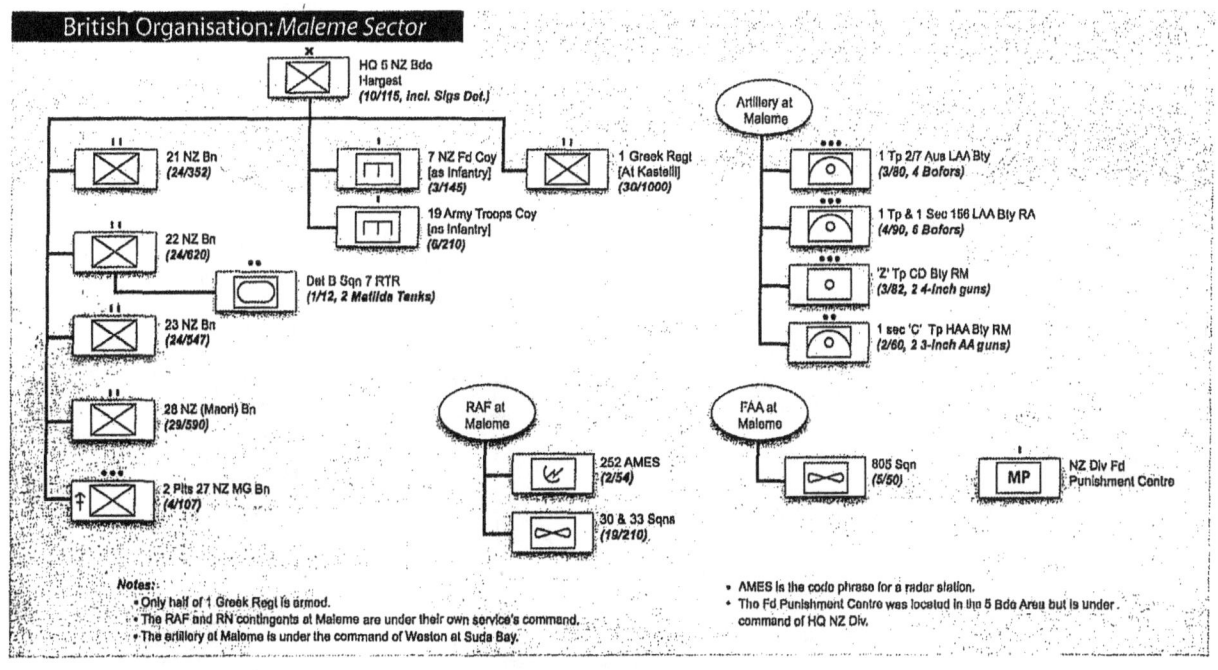

Source: *Battle of Crete*, Albert Palazzo, pg 33

APPENDIX R: Retimo and Heraklion Sector Task Organizations

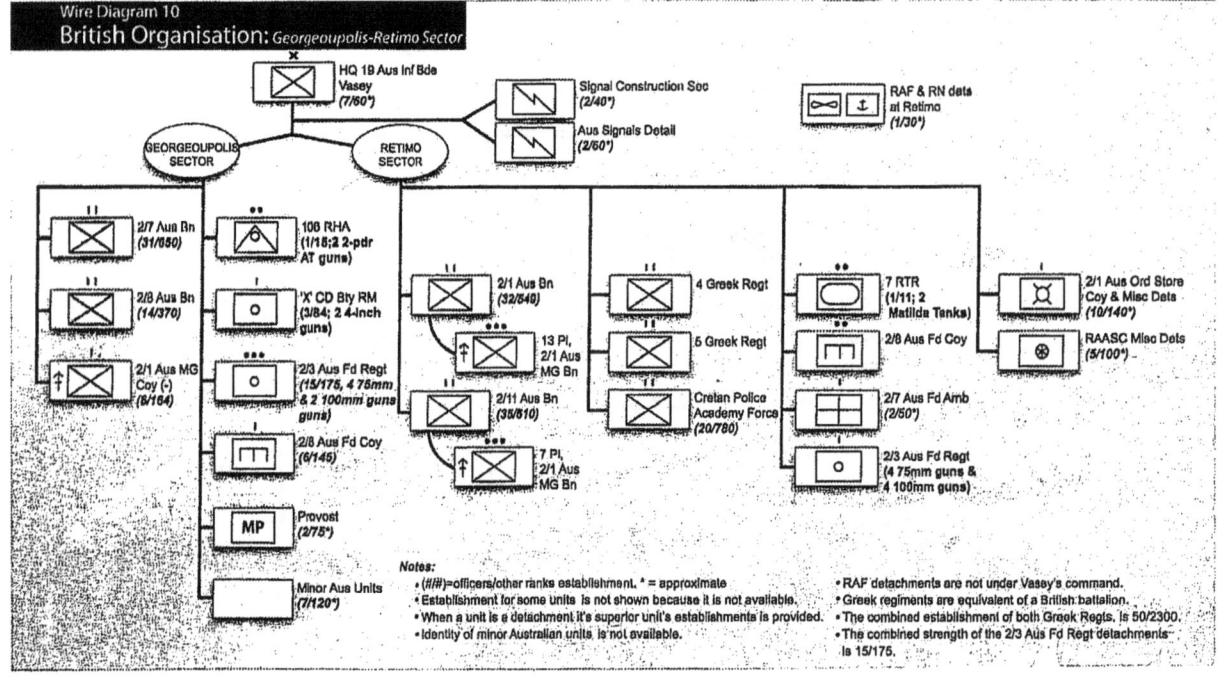

Source: *Battle of Crete*, Albert Palazzo, pg 87

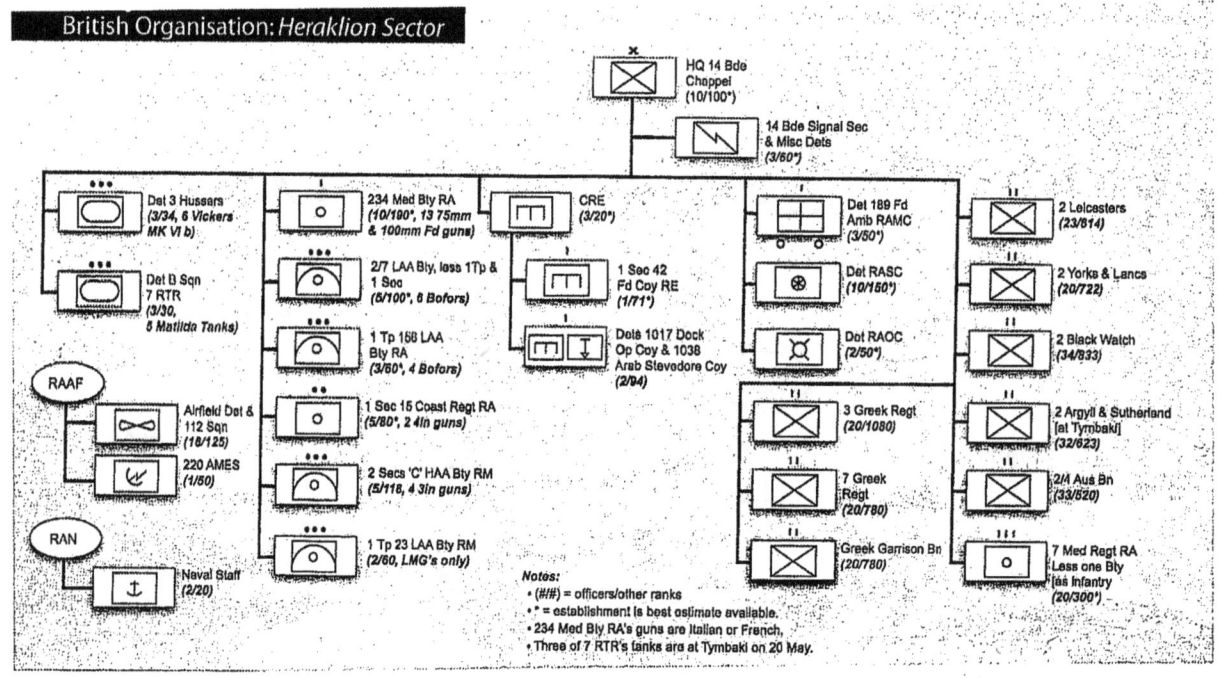

Source: *Battle of Crete*, Albert Palazzo, pg 75

APPENDIX S: Operation Mercury

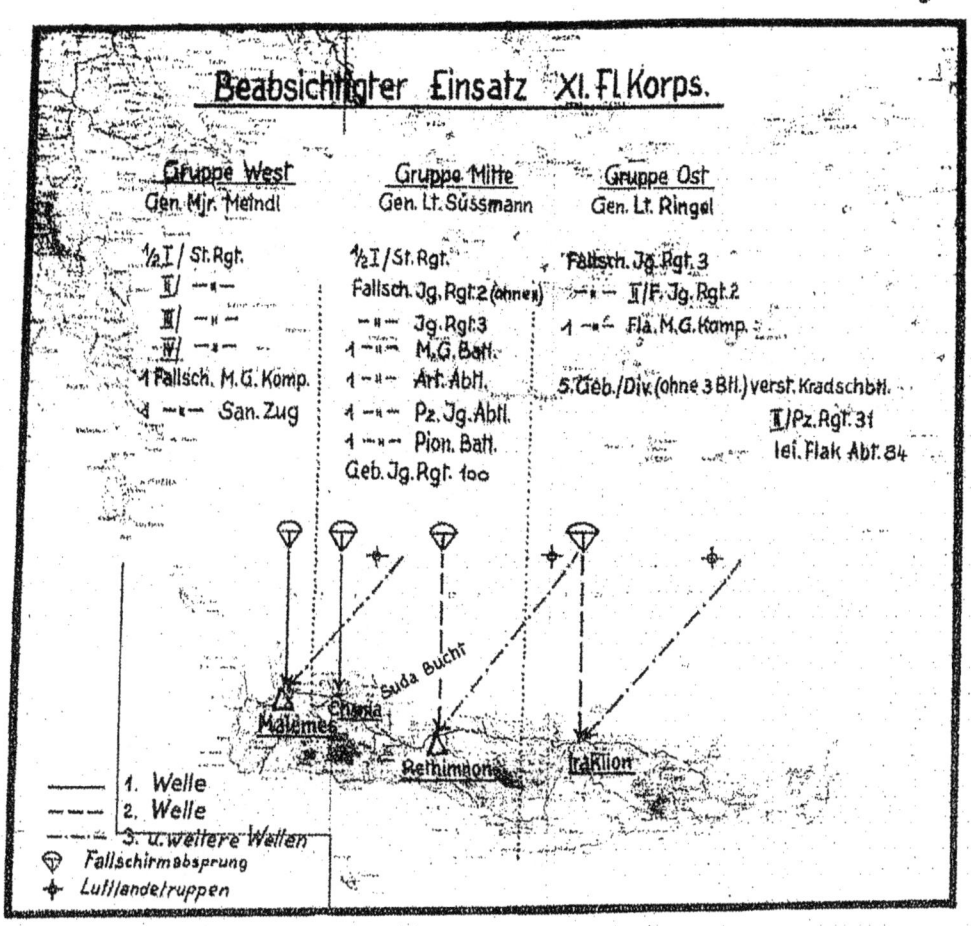

Source: *Battle of Crete*, Albert Palazzo, pg 30

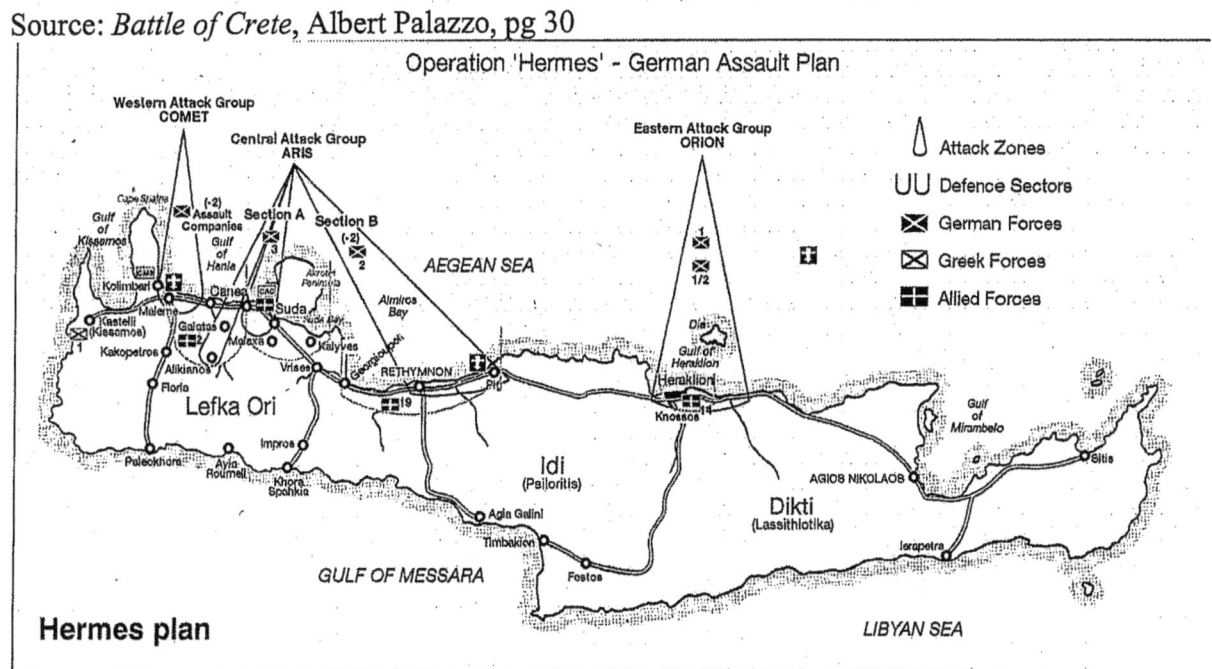

Source: *Battle of Crete*, George Forty, pg 74

APPENDIX T: Attack Maps

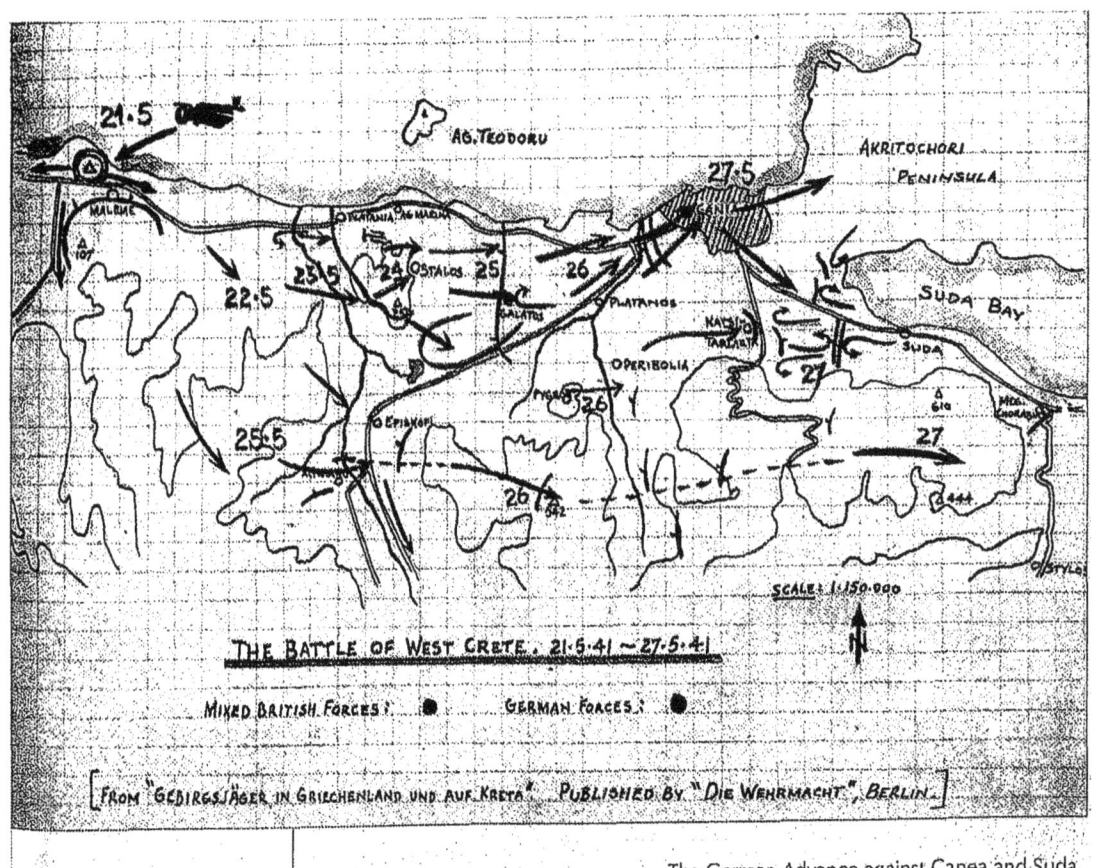

The German Advance against Canea and Suda.
Australian War Memorial RC02708

Source: *Battle of Crete*, Albert Palazzo, pg 113

APPENDIX T (cont.): Attack Maps

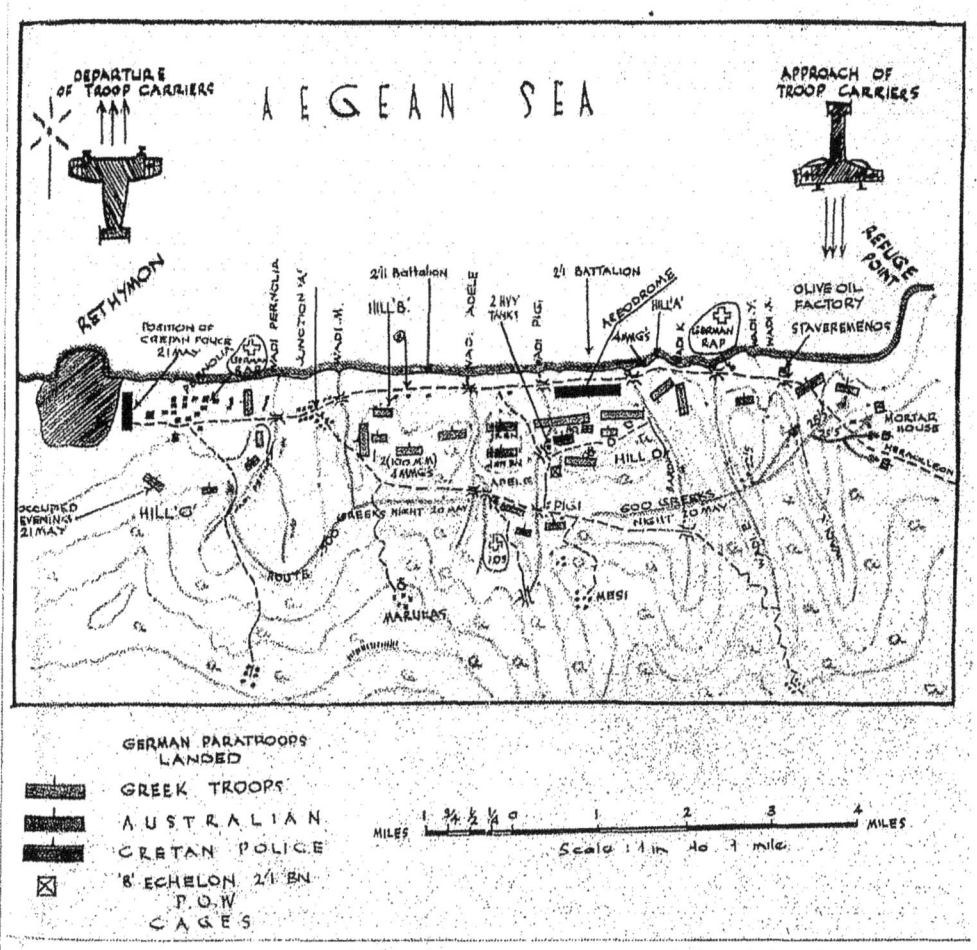

Map showing the German Approach Route and the Australian and Greek Positions.
Australian War Memorial Map Collection

Source: *Battle of Crete*, Albert Palazzo, pg 101

APPENDIX U: Royal Navy Defense

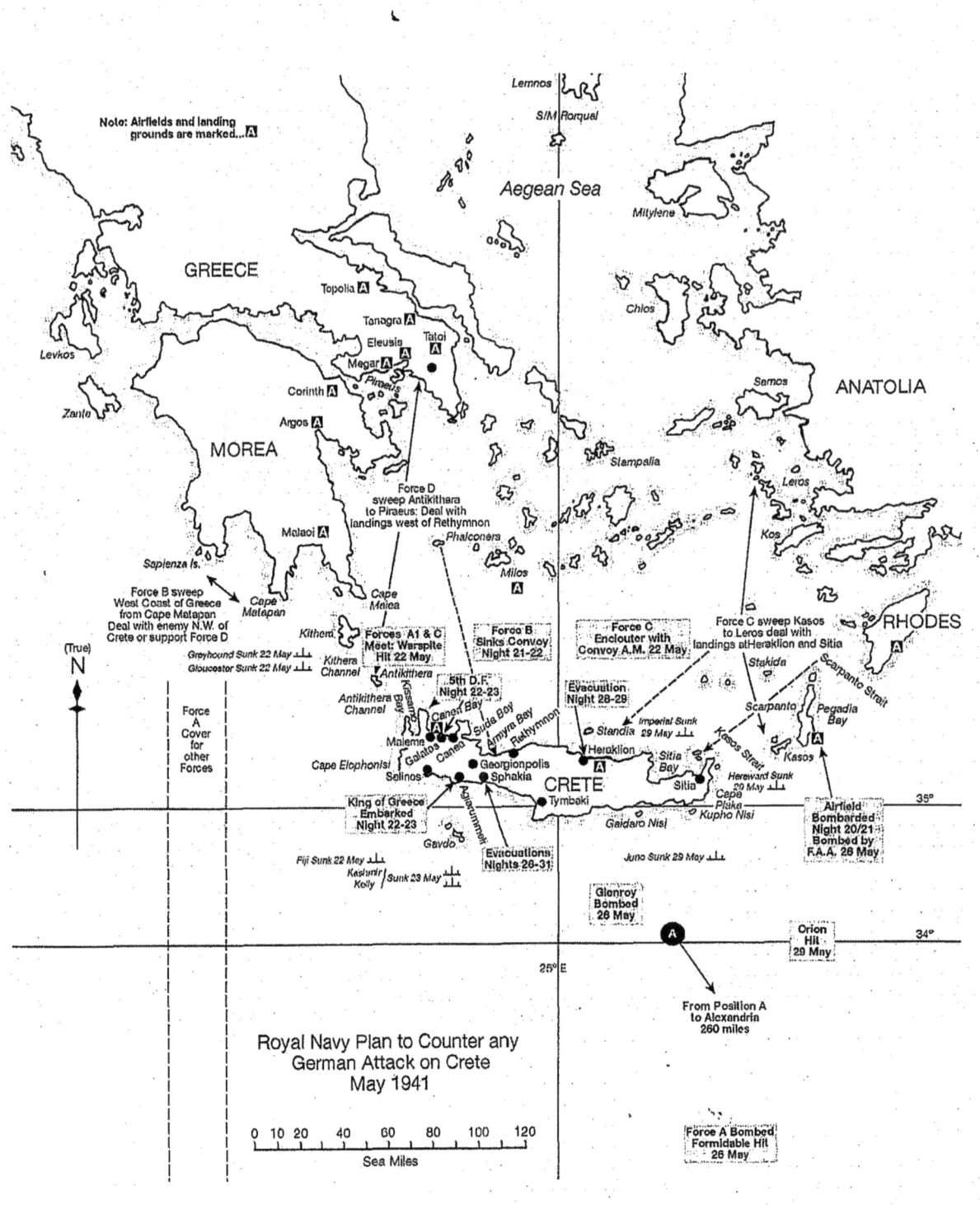

Source: *Battle of Crete*, George Forty, pg 63

APPENDIX V: Royal Navy Loses

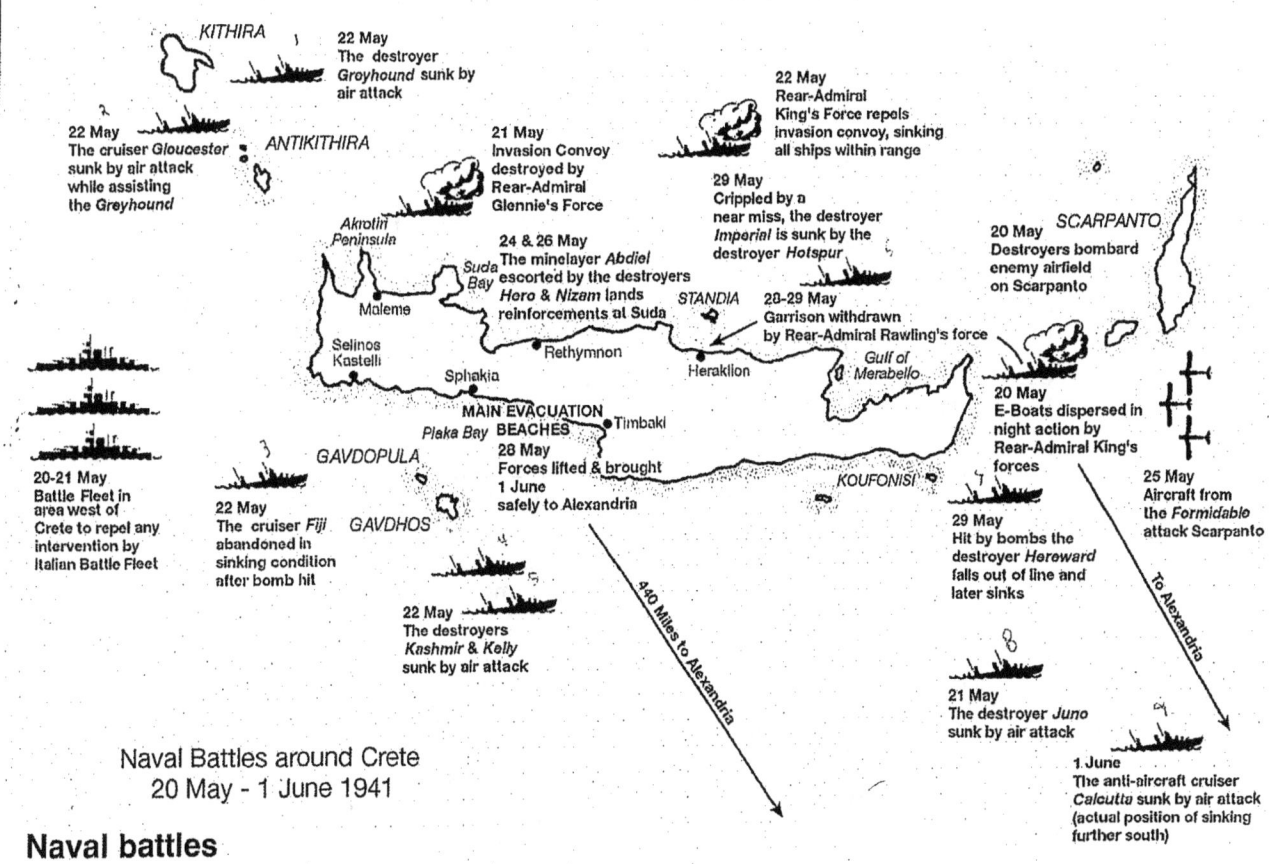

Naval Battles around Crete
20 May - 1 June 1941

Naval battles

Source: *Battle of Crete*, George Forty, pg 112

APPENDIX V (cont.): Royal Navy Loses

Royal Navy Losses during Crete Campaign

- Unless otherwise noted ships are HMS.
- Table does not include the loss of minor vessels.

Date	Ship	Type	Fate	Out of Action
21 May	Juno	Destroyer	Sunk	
21 May	Ajax	Light Cruiser	Damaged	minor damage
22 May	Gloucester	Light Cruiser	Sunk	
22 May	Fiji	Light Cruiser	Sunk	
22 May	Naiad	Light Cruiser	Damaged	3 weeks
22 May	Valiant	Battleship	Damaged	Not out of action
22 May	Warspite	Battleship	Damaged	7 months
22 May	Carlisle	Anti-Aircraft Cruiser	Damaged	1 month
22 May	Greyhound	Destroyer	Sunk	
22 May	Kingston	Destroyer	Damaged	1 week
23 May	Kashmir	Destroyer	Sunk	
23 May	Kelly	Destroyer	Sunk	
23 May	Ilex	Destroyer	Damaged	4 days
23 May	Havock	Destroyer	Damaged	3 weeks
26 May	Formidable	Carrier	Damaged	6 months
26 May	Nubian	Destroyer	Damaged	17 months
26 May	Glenroy	Assault Ship	Damaged	minor
27 May	Barham	Battleship	Damaged	2 months
28 May	Ajax	Light Cruiser	Damaged	3 months
29 May	Imperial	Destroyer	Sunk	
29 May	Hereward	Destroyer	Sunk	
29 May	Dido	Light Cruiser	Damaged	5 months
29 May	Orion	Light Cruiser	Damaged	8.5 months
29 May	Decoy	Destroyer	Damaged	
29 May	HMAS Nizam	Destroyer	Damaged	1 week
30 May	HMAS Perth	Light Cruiser	Damaged	4.5 months
30 May	Kelvin	Destroyer	Damaged	6.5 months
31 May	HMAS Napier	Destroyer	Damaged	1 week
31 May	Calcutta	Anti-Aircraft Cruiser	Sunk	

Source: *Battle of Crete*, Albert Palazzo, pg 148

APPENDIX W: German Forced Landings on Maleme

Source: *Battle of Crete*, George Forty, pg 95

APPENDIX X: Cretan Resistance and the SOE

After the German victory, SOE agents, Capt. John D.S. Pendlebury,[98] Jack Smith-Hughes,[99] Capt. Patrick M. Leigh Fermor,[100] Capt. A.W. Xan Fielding,[101] and many others, assisted the Cretan resistance. By using the already well-developed Cretan network they provided safe passage off the island to hundreds of Allied service members trapped behind enemy lines or who had escaped from POW camps. In the following four years of German occupation, SOE agents continued to train and develop Cretan resistance groups lead by Kapetan Manoli Bandooras, George Petrakageorgis and Antonis Girgorakis, better known as Satanas.[102] The SOE trained resistance roamed the mountains and rural villages of Crete providing security to the population, sheltering Allied soldiers and attacking the Germans whenever the opportunity arose. In fact, partisan attacks were so predictable and vicious the Germans restricted their defensive efforts to the urban population centers, moving into the countryside only in force.[103]

Throughout the battle and the following resistance the Cretan miltia, Gendarmarine, Partisans and civilians fought gallantly. They often fought with rocks, rakes, shovels and knives defending their homes and their countryside to the last drop of their blood.[104] As described by the glass-eyed Pendlebury, "the Cretans have a warlike spirit...given the weapons...the Cretans could defeat a German invasion virtually on their own."[105] Unfortunately, the Allies denied them weapons, uniforms and proper support. Allied commanders treated them as a nuisance, placed them in precarious defensive positions,[106] and left them to scrounge weapons from the Germans they killed. Yet, they fought valiantly and remained loyal to the Allies. Had Freyberg or his subordinates attempted to organize and integrate these volunteers the battle may well have turned. The results will remain unknown; however, the Allies unreasonably dismissed the opportunity.

APPENDIX Y: A Sketch of Major General Sir Bernard Cyril Freyberg's Leadership

Major General Bernard Cyril Freyberg is arguably New Zealand's most celebrated soldier and military commander. His exploits during World War I earned him the reputation as "the top tactical commander."[107] He entered WW I as a company commander at Antwerp and ended the war highly decorated Brigade Commander nominated for Brigadier General as the result of his performances at Gallipoli, Somme, and Flanders. World War II found him medically unfit to serve in the British Army; however, New Zealand offered him command of the 2nd New Zealand Expeditionary Force. After accepting command, Freyberg and the 2nd NZ shipped off to Egypt where he and his Division would acquit themselves well in the Greece, North Africa and Italian campaigns. Churchhill and Freyberg's superiors sought his tactical and operational prowess[108], his knack for training was the envy of his peers[109], and his informal manner, warrior ethos, and unflappable courage caused his soldiers to revere him. The Battle of Crete was the only blemish on Freyberg's otherwise distinguished military career.[110]

BACKGROUND

Freyberg was born in 1889, in the London suburb of Richmond, England.. At the age of two, he and his parents moved to New Zealand. Freyberg remained relatively anonymous until after he graduated from Wellington College, New Zealand in 1904. After graduating, he continued his studies to become a dentist and during this time he began swimming competitively. In 1906 and 1910 he won the New Zealand 100-yard championship. In 1911 he was licensed as a practicing dentist and became a subaltern in the Morrinsville Territorial Army until 1914. Evidently unchallenged by civilian pursuits and unable to earn a king's commission, Freyberg departed New Zealand for England where he would petition for a commission in the British Army.

Freyberg's arrival in England coincided with Britain's entry into WW I and his efforts to earn a British Army commission lead him to Britain's first Lord of the Admiralty, then Sir Winston Leonard Spencer Churchill. Freyberg's efforts to persuade Churchill earned him a commission in the Hood Battalion of the Royal Naval Division and Churchill's continued audience for the remainder of his career. It is not clear if Freyberg and Churchill remained in close contact in the years proceeding his appointment as the CreForce (the unit designation for all Allied forces on Crete) Commander, or if his performance on the battlefields of WWI are what made such an indelible impression on Churchill.[111] However, prior to personally appointing him as CreForce Commander, Churchill described Freyberg as a man who would "fight for King and Country with an unconquerable heart anywhere he is ordered, and with whatever forces he is given by superior authorities, and he [thus] imparts his own invincible firmness of mind to all around him." [112]

THE GREAT WAR

His accomplishments and heroics while serving the Hood Battalion during WW I served to boost his reputation as a courageous leader who led from the front. Freyberg first served as a company commander at Antwerp in 1914 and then at Gallipoli in 1915. At Gallipoli, Freyberg put his championship swimming skills to work and there he became a legend. During the initial assaults, Freyberg swam ashore in the Dardanelles to light false beacons as part of a plan to disguise the chosen landing beaches, an act for which he received the Distinguished Service

Order (DSO).[113] Following Gallipoli, Freyberg served on the Western Front, in particular at the Battle of the Somme. There he was wounded four times, once severely, in a twenty-four hour period[114] and was awarded the Victoria Cross (VC) for leading the Hood Battalion to capture Beaucourt in Flanders.[115] By the end of WWI, Freyberg had built a larger than life reputation. At the age of 28, he was the youngest general officer and had been wounded nine times, won the VC, and the DSO with two bars.[116] Buildings and streets in New Zealand were named after him and his statue was erected in Wellington.[117]

THE WAR TO END ALL WARS

Prior to WWII Freyberg returned to his substantive rank of lieutenant-colonel and then medically retired from the British Army; however, he was offered command of the 2nd New Zealand Expeditionary Force, by the New Zealand government. Shortly after taking the reins of his newly formed command, Freyberg and his division traveled to Egypt to join Field Marshal Archibald Wavell's Middle East Command. Freyberg fought his initial battle of WWII in the Battle of Greece as part of the 1st Australian Corps. However, by the time his unit consolidated and deployed to Greece, they faced the overwhelming German onslaught and fought a withdrawal to the Aegean. According to General Wavell, the withdrawal could not have been carried out as well by any other Division.[118] From Greece, Freyberg and portions of his division would land on Crete, where Freyberg accepted the dubious honor of scraping together a defense with meager time, resources, or assistance. While at Crete, Freyberg suffered a sound defeat at the hands of the *Luftwaffe* and *11th Fliegerkorps*. Undeterred by this defeat, Freyberg reorganized and refitted his 2nd New Zealand Division in Egypt and went on to persevere under Field Marshal Bernard Law Montgomery in North Africa and the Italian campaigns. There, Freyberg continued to shine in Operation Supercharge at Alamein and Operation Supercharge II at Tebaga Gap. Freyberg reached the rank of Lieutenant-General and received a third bar for his DSO before WWII's final days.

THE BLEMISH

It is easy to identify Freyberg's personal courage and tactical prowess as a young officer in WWI, and one can appreciate the operational and strategic skill, leadership, and competence he must have demonstrated in order to remain successful as a division commander throughout WWII. However, as the CreForce Commander at the Battle of Crete, he failed to create an effective command. This may have been caused by the many complexities surrounding the situation on Crete before Freyberg arrived. Of these, the main complexities were Britain's inability to conduct complimentary operations between the Royal Navy, Royal Air Force, and the Army[119] and an overall lack of defensive preparations on the island.[120] Another factor that may explain Freyberg's inability to overcome the situation and succeed, may be based in two of his personal characteristics – obstinacy and extreme reluctance to criticize.[121]

Freyberg's most notable mistake comes from his inability to believe intelligence reports from Churchill's super secret decoding establishment, ULTRA[122], that the Germans would attack Crete through an airborne assault. Through ULTRA, the British and Freyberg had learned the entire operational plan for Operation Mercury, the German assault plan. They knew the dates, the times, the units, the objectives, and the manpower involved.[123] However, most likely due to his conventional background and previous experiences, Freyberg was unable to accept a different approach and maintained that the assault would come from the sea.[124] This mistake led to the misplacement of the Allied defenses and placed already scarce, valuable equipment, artillery, and heavy weapons, in positions unable to influence the initial stages of the assault. Likewise, the defensive positions were placed forward or inside of the intended German landing zones.[125] Consequently, when the *Fallschirmjäger* began to land inside and behind the Allied positions units became disoriented; thus, creating significant communications problems which caused some units to incorrectly assume that they'd become isolated and as a result they chose to fall back.

Aside from misjudging the axis of the assaults, Freyberg was unable to formulate a joint approach to further the defense of Crete or create a unified ground defense. The paramount obstacle to creating a joint approach to the island's defense was General Wavell's focus on North Africa operations.[126] Wavell's Middle East Command siphoned off much needed resources, leaving the Cretan defense lacking the firepower to deny large-scale, determined attacks. Most notably, CreForce received only token RAF support throughout the battle. In turn, the *Luftwaffe* was able to command the ground from the sky.[127] Freyberg seemed to accept his lack of resources and equipment and refrained from demanding greater Air Force support or that Wavell allocate of more resources. Instead, Freyberg seemed committed to "fight for King and Country with an unconquerable heart anywhere he is ordered, and with whatever forces he is given by superior authority."[128]

Freyberg was equally as undemanding of his subordinates. Freyberg took command of CreForce from Major-General Eric C. Weston who had previously commanded the Mobile Naval Base Defense Organization (MNDBO). When Weston left to return to MNDBO, a subordinate of CreForce, he took the CreForce staff with him, leaving Freyberg, the Commander of CreForce, with a driver and a few orderlies.[129] Freyberg's inability to confront Weston left Freyberg and CreForce with an insufficient and untrained staff. Likewise, Freyberg would struggle to maintain situational awareness, as well as command and control throughout the battle.

Freyberg divided the island into five defensible sectors, placing a headquarters in each sector.[130] However, three of the sectors were comprised of units from one division, which Freyberg allowed the division commander to retain command and control of all three sectors. This allowed the division commander to reinforce any of his three sectors without taking into consideration the situations that might be developing across the island. Consequently, Freyberg was unable to coordinate a timely response to German assaults because the division commander elsewhere had already committed the reserve force in that sector.

CONCLUSION

History does support that Freyberg, through his obstinacy, ignored "perfect" intelligence and failed to coordinate a synchronous defense thereby costing the Allies the Battle of Crete. However, in the instance of Crete, the strategic miscalculations and ill allocation of time and resources likely had a greater impact on the outcome at Crete. Therefore, Freyberg's otherwise distinguished military career, both before and after the Battle of Crete, should not be viewed as anything but that. He distinguished himself through personal courage, heroism, and bravery as a tactical and operational commander throughout WWI. He again distinguished himself as an effective leader and war-fighter in operational and strategic warfare throughout WWII. He was an effective and charismatic leader whose only blemish was the Battle of Crete, where he willingly accepted a less than optimal situation and attempted to bring victory through insurmountable complexities.

Notes

1. Gerhard Schreiber, Bernd Stegemann, and Detlef Vogel. *Germany and the Second World War: Volume III: The Mediterranean, South-East Europe, and North Africa 1939-1941 From Italy's Declaration of Non-Belligerence ... the War*. (New York: Oxford University Press, USA, 1995), 451-453

2. Craig A. Swanson, 28 November 2007, Operation Husky discussion, Marine Corps University (28 November 2007).

3. Martin Gilbert. *Winston S. Churchill Finest Hour Volume VI*. (Boston: Houghton Mifflin Company, 1983), 882-885, 899

4. Ibid., 904-905

5. D.N. Davin. *Crete*. (Wellington: War History Branch, 1953), 4-7; Palazzo, Albert *Battle of Crete*. (Canberra: Army History Unit, 2007), 158 ; Gilbert, 898-900

6. Gilbert, 884-5, 904-907, 1064-1093; Davin, 11-20

7. George Forty. *Battle of Crete*. (Hersham: Ian Allan Publishing, 2002), 18-19; Davin, 30-39, 42-53; Palazzo, 13-15; Gilbert, 1073-1093

8. Davin, 14-17, 21-23; Palazzo, 13-15

9. Palazzo, 146-154; Forty 18

10. Davin, 46; Forty, 52

11. Beevor, Antony. *Crete: The Battle and the Resistance*. (Oxford: Westview Press, 1994), 55, 60, 66, 177-189; Kiriakopoulos, G. C.. *Ten Days to Destiny: The Battle for Crete 1941*. (New York: Watt, 1985), 76-79

12. Davin, 88-241; Kiriakopoulos, 119-220; Schreiber, 550-555

13. Palazzo, 149-152; Forty, 107-118

14. Schreiber, 342-355

15. Forty, 15

16. Gilbert, 922

17. Ibid, 921-924

18. Schreiber, 451-53: Gilbert, 876, 884-5, 898

Notes

19. D.N. Davin. *Crete*. (Wellington: War History Branch, 1953), 3 Schrieber, 452:

20. Gilbert, 451-478, 891-911, 952-967

21. Schreiber, 451-453

22. Ibid., 451-478, 529-532

23. Forty, 18

24. Palazzo, 147

25. Kiriakopoulos, 10-13

26. Beevor, 5

27. Schreiber, 454-58, 469; Kiriakopoulos, 14; Davin, 3

28. Schreiber, 468-70

29. Kiriakopoulos, 14; Davin, 5; Gilbert, 898; Schreiber, 531

30. Palazzo, 9; Schreiber, 451-453

31. Gilbert, 611-612; Palazzo, 25

32. Beevor, 14; Schreiber, 531

33. Beevor, 16

34. Schreiber, 469; Gilbert, 899

35. Schreiber, 527

36. Ibid., 470

37. Davin, 6

38. Forty, 8

39. Gilbert, 904

40. Ibid., 905

Notes

41. Ibid., 905

42. Ibid., 899

43. Ibid., 899

44. Ibid., 899

45. Beevor, 16

46. Davin, 5

47. Gilbert, 907

48. Gilbert, 1065, 1072; Davin, 7; Forty, 15

49. Gilbert, 1058-1079; Davin, 22-38

50. Palazzo, 147

51. Davin, 22

52. Davin, 22-30

53. Palazzo, 13-15; Gilbert, 1110

54. Beevor, 84; Schreiber, 469; Gilbert, 899

55. Palazzo, 13

56. Palazzo, 13-15; Davin, 12

57. Palazzo, 14

58. Ibid., 14

59. Davin, 12

60. Ibid., 12, 16

61. Palazzo, 25; Gilbert, 1085, 1088, 1089

62. Davin 15, Palazzo 14

Notes

63. Davin, 14-19

64. Gilbert, 905

65. Davin, 20

66. Ibid., 10

67. Palazzo, 15; Davin 8-10

68. Palazzo, 156; Davin, 20

69. Forty, 101

70. Davin, 138; Kiriakopoulos, 183-185

71. Forty, 101

72. Kiriakopoulos, 78, 148, 186

73. Ibid., 159

74. Beevor, 96

75. Palazzo, 154

76. Palazzo, 146-7

77. Schreiber, 541-548

78. Palazzo, 152

79. Ibid., 156

80. Palazzo 33, 53, 55, 57, 75, 87; Davin, 23, 46

81. Davin, 25-6

82. Palazzo 17

83. Davin, 39-42; Forty, 40-42, Palazzo, 17-19

84. Palazzo, 17-18

Notes

85. Davin, 22-3

86. Ibid., 28

87. Palazzo, 20

88. Palazzo, 25; Gilbert, 1085, 1088, 1089

89. Gilbert, 1085

90. Palazzo, 25

91. Davin, 31

92. Kiriakopoulos, 108

93. Palazzo, 19; Davin, 22-87

94. Palazzo, 32

95. Palazzo, 19, Davin, 22-87

96. Davin, 46; Schreiber, 543-555; Forty, 52

97. Gilbert, 1099

98. Beevor, 96-8, 140-2, 179, 226

99. Ibid., 223-4, 242-4

100. Beevor, 9-10, 76, 96, 288-9, 291-3, 301-11, 330-1

101. Forty, 158; Beevor, 245-6, 250-1, 281-2, 299, 331, 335

102. Forty, 157; Beevor, 97

103. Beevor, 330

104. Beevor, 177-189

105. Ibid, 27

106. Kiriakopoulos, 78

Notes

107. Palazzo, 18

108. Beevor, 82-84

109. Forty, 40-41; Beevor, 83

110. Palazzo, 18; Forty, 40-41, Beevor, 82

111. Kiriakopoulos, 68-69; Palazzo, 15-19

112. Kiriakopoulos, 60

113. Forty, 40-41; Palazzo, 18,

114. Palazzo, 18

115. Beevor, 82-83

116. Forty, 40-41; Palazzo, 18; Beevor 82-83

117. Palazzo, 41

118. Davin, 40; Forty, 42

119. Gilbert, 905; Palazzo, 22-23

120. Davin, 8-10, 20; Palazzo, 15

121. Beevor, 83

122. Palazzo, 25

123. Palazzo, 25; Gilbert, 1085, 1088, 1089; Kiriakopoulos, 108

124. Palazzo, 25

125. Palazzo, 39, 67, 77, 84, 89, 97, 101

126. Schreiber, 469; Beevor, 84; Gilbert, 89

127. Palazzo, 154-158, 162; Forty, 59-62

128. Kiriakopoulos, 60

Notes

129. Davin, 41; Palazzo, 17-18, Beevor, 85-86; Kiriakopoulos, 62-64

130. Palazzo, 26-28

Bibliography

Antill, Peter. *Crete 1941: Germany's lightning airborne assault (Campaign)*. Oxford: Osprey Publishing, 2005.

Beevor, Antony. *Crete: The Battle and the Resistance (History and Warfare)*. Oxford: Westview Press, 1994.

Buckley, Christopher. *Greece and Crete 1941*. New York City: Efstathiadis Group, Greece, 1984.

Davin, D.N. . *Crete*. Wellington: War History Branch, 1953.

Forty, George. *Battle of Crete*. Hersham: Ian Allan Publishing, 2002.

Freyberg, Paul. *Bernard Freyberg, Vc: Soldier of Two Nations*. Great Britain : Hodder & Stoughton, 1992.

Gilbert, Martin. *Winston S. Churchill Finest Hour Volume VI*. Boston: Houghton Mifflin Company, 1983.

Kiriakopoulos, G. C.. *ten Days to Destiny: The Battle for Crete 1941*. New York: Watt, 1985.

Palazzo, Albert . *Battle of Crete* . Canberra: Army History Unit, 2007.

Paul, E.V. . *Battle for Crete*. Wellington: Army Board, 1943.

Schreiber, Gerhard, Bernd Stegemann, and Detlef Vogel. *Germany and the Second World War: Volume III: The Mediterranean, South-East Europe, and North Africa 1939-1941 (From Italy's Declaration of Non-Belligerence ... the War) (Germany and the Second World War)*. New York: Oxford University Press, USA, 1995.

The Battle of Crete - May 1941. Ft. Leavenworth: Hellenic Army General Staff, 2000.

www.ingramcontent.com/pod-product-compliance
Lightning Source LLC
Chambersburg PA
CBHW081259170426
43198CB00017B/2850